THREE WARFARES

JOHN ARCOVIO

FOREWORD BY TEKLEMARIAM GEZAHEGNE

Cover artwork by Nick LeGuern

All scripture quotations are from the New King James Version of the Bible. Bold and italic type are for author's emphasis only.

All Hebrew and Greek translations of biblical terms are taken from *Strong's Hebrew and Greek Lexicon.*

Three Warfares by John Arcovio
© 1996
Published by Spirit Led Ministries, Inc.
3422 W. Hammer Lane, Suite C-289
Stockton, CA 95219
(209) 608-3399
(209)478-8972 fax

Visit our website at http://www.spiritled.org

ISBN 0-9647343-0-1

Printed in the United States of America.
First edition July 1995
Reprinted;
July 1996
November 1998

See back page of book for order form

TABLE OF CONTENTS

ACKNOWLEDGMENTS

First, I want to give Jesus thanks and all honor and glory for His strength and infinite wisdom in allowing me to write this humble book. All I have and all I am is because of Him!

I thank my lovely wife, Andrea, for being incredibly supportive and terrific. Thank you for bringing our son into this world. I love you and could not make it without you!

I thank Terry Cheever from DeRidder, Louisiana, for her help in typing this book and my dear friend, Brother Leroy Kelly for allowing me the extra time during revival to finish this book.

Thank you, "Papa" Billy Cole, for faithfully preaching the principles upon which much of this book is based. May this simple effort honor you.

May the Lord richly bless all of you. This would not be possible without you!

PREFACE

This book, *Three Warfares,* is essential for those serious about defeating the giants of our age. It is not intended for those satisfied with living a "status quo" Christian life. It is intended for those spiritual warriors who have sold out for the cause of Christ! Our simple prayer is that we will challenge all blessed by this handbook of warfare to step onto the battlefield of the **Lion**, of the **Bear** and of the **Goliath** of our age!

May the Lord richly bless you.

Rev. John Arcovio

FOREWORD

We are living in the time of the fulfillment of all biblical prophecies. God is seeking vessels that He can move through to fulfill these prophecies. This will be accomplished through prayer and fasting.

God is raising men to stir and create a great hunger for apostolic revival. Isaiah 49:5-7 records,

Now the Lord says, who formed me from the womb to be his servant, to bring Jacob back to Him, So that Israel is gathered to Him (For I shall be glorious in the eyes of the Lord, and my God shall be my strength), Indeed He says, It is too small a thing that You should be my servant to raise up the tribes of Jacob, And to restore the preserved ones of Israel; I will also give You as a light to the Gentiles, That You should be My salvation to the ends of the earth. Thus says the Lord, The Redeemer of Israel, their Holy One, To Him whom man despises, To Him whom the nation abhors, To the Servant of rulers: Kings shall see and arise, Princes also shall worship, Because of the Lord who is faithful, The Holy One of Israel; And He has chosen You.

This is the mystery of God which He will fulfill through His called and chosen instruments. Isaiah 66:18-21 says,

> For I know their works and their thoughts. It shall be that I will gather all nations and tongues; and they shall come and see My glory. I will set a sign among them; and those among them who escape I will send to the nations: to Tarshish and Pul and Lud, who draw the bow, and Tubal and Javan, to the coast lands afar off who have not heard My fame nor seen My glory. And they shall declare My glory among the Gentiles. Then they shall bring all your brethren for an offering to the Lord out of all nations, on horses and in chariots and in litters, on mules and on camels, to My holy mountain Jerusalem, says the Lord, as the children of Israel bring an offering in a clean vessel into the house of the Lord. And I will also take some of them for priests and Levites, says the Lord.

Daily, thousands are waking up and opening their hearts to God, allowing Him to accomplish these prophecies through them. I appreciate Brother Arcovio, for I feel he is one of these who, through fasting and prayer, has opened his heart to allow God to give him an understanding of these prophecies. The Lord is using this Man of God in this last hour in a mighty way.

You will be challenged by the truths he has written in this book.

Rev. Teklemariam Gezahagne

10

SCRIPTURE TEXT

"For we do not wrestle against flesh and blood, but against principalities, against powers, against the rulers of the darkness of this age, against spiritual hosts of wickedness in the heavenly places" (Ephesians 6:12).

INTRODUCTION TO THE WARFARES

On a quiet, low valley the lone figure of a giant is seen making his way across the field. Suddenly his husky voice, shouting taunts, jeers, obscenities and boastful challenges, shatters the silence and causes men across the way to cower in their tents. As has occurred many times before, the men do not respond; rather they look at each other, waiting for someone to make a move.

Accepting the challenge, a young man moves swiftly across the field to face this giant who has dared to defy the armies of the living God. Who is this brave youth? How did he happen to have such strength and courage while thousands of others much older and more able and experienced stood by to watch?

As we look at the three warfares this young man faced, we will discover what it was that so swiftly matured and equipped him.

Page 14 is the Map of Elah

The Valley of Elah

Map created with Logos Bible Atlas, Copyright © 1994 Logos Research Systems, Inc.

ELAH (Heb. Ñe,,la,, 'terebinth'). A valley used by the Philistines to gain access to Central Palestine. It was the scene of David's victory over Goliath (I Samuel 17:2; 21:9), and is generally identified with the modern Wadi es-Sant, 18 kilometers southwest of Jerusalem. J.D.D.

1

THE LION: WARFARE OF THE FLESH

David sat quietly on a grassy hillside just outside Bethlehem, watching his father's sheep. The wind blew softly through the dry shrubs surrounding him as he watched the sheep peacefully grazing below. His thoughts shifted to his love and desire to worship and serve his beloved Jehovah. He reached for his harp and soon the flowing chords of adoration and praise drifted down the hillside, mixing in perfect harmony with the chirping of the birds and the many other melodious sounds of creation surrounding him.

David's father trusted him with the sheep, for David was a loyal, hardworking young man. He was content in fulfilling whatever task his father asked him to do on the homestead, though he always felt a sense of a higher calling that he could not put his finger on. Nevertheless, he did not neglect his duties while daydreaming about some plan that Jehovah might have for his life.

Suddenly the harmony was shattered by the thunderous roar of a lion that had crept up unawares. The fearsome sound brought David instantly to his feet. As David reached for his sling, the lion sprang forward, trapping a lamb against a rock. David knew he would not have time to load a stone into his sling and get a clear shot, so he picked up his staff and charged forward, waving it and yelling. He was acting upon his fierce loyalty for the sheep with no regard for his own safety. The lion rose to face him, growling menacingly.

"Lord Jehovah, be my strength and protection right now," David whispered breathlessly. As the lion moved closer, David reached into his cloak and pulled out the saber he kept concealed there. Unexpectedly, the lion crouched and sprang forward, snarling and with his claws extended. David rushed forward to meet the lion's attack as a strength and courage he had never felt before compelled him. Grabbing the lion by the beard with one hand, David smote the lion with the saber with the other, using all the strength that he had. The lion roared with anger and tried to twist out of David's grasp. Nevertheless, David swung the saber repeatedly until the lion lay lifeless at his feet.

David fell to his knees trembling for he knew he had just experienced the delivering hand of the Jehovah God of Israel. While on his knees he thanked and worshiped God a long while before rising to lead the sheep on the long trail home.

"How the mighty have fallen, and the weapons of war perished!" (II Samuel 1:27).

Just as David had to face and defeat his lion to prepare him for a much greater battle ahead, we will have to face our spiritual lion and defeat it before we can move on to experience warfare in a higher dimension. The only way we can be assured victory is if we make sure our spiritual weapons remain intact and in use.

All spiritual wars won in this natural realm are first won in the supernatural realm of fasting and prayer.

"For though we walk in the flesh, we do not war according to the flesh. For the weapons of our warfare are not carnal, but mighty through God for pulling down strongholds..." (II Corinthians 10:3-4).

When we decide to be a vessel used by God to affect apostolic revival through spiritual warfare, we will first face the **warfare of the lion of our flesh.** We must never overlook this dimension of warfare! We must have the lion skin of our flesh hanging on the walls of our spiritual house.

"For we do not wrestle against flesh and blood, but against ...the rulers of the darkness of this age..." (Ephesians 6:12).

Paul classified the first dimension of warfare as rulers of the darkness of this age that cause spiritual wickedness in high places. *Rulers* is translated from *kosmokrator (kos-mok-rat'-ore),* and is defined as "lord of the world, devil and demons." These are the everyday demons of lust, envy, strife, jealousy, murder, hate, etc. that feed on carnal flesh.

I have written to you, fathers, Because you have known Him who is from the beginning. I have written to you, young men, Because you are strong, and the word of God abides in you, and you have overcome the wicked one. Do not love the world or the things in the world. If anyone loves the world, the love of the Father is not in him. For all that is in the world—the lust of the flesh, the lust of the eyes, and the pride of life—is not of the Father but is of the world. And the world is passing away, and the lust of it; but he who does the will of God abides forever (I John 2:14-17).

When we have allowed our minds to become washed by the water of God's Word, when our spirits become strengthened through praying and fasting, and when we have a desire to turn toward Jesus through intimate conversation and relationship, then we are truly ready to face and deal with the "lions of our flesh." Overcoming a lion simply through strong "will power" is impossible. We deal with the lions of this life through a relationship with Jesus Christ, who is the true Lion of the Tribe of Judah (Revelation 5:5).

There is nothing like a one-to-three-day fast to deal with the lions of our flesh. I fully believe that when the person fasts from one to three days he is strictly dealing with the lion of his flesh. It is not just simply the work of fasting or the work of prayer that causes the lion of our flesh to become subdued; it is subdued only when fasting and prayer are done with that intimate longing, desire and hunger to draw closer to Jesus. To be more like Him. To emanate His character and His love. To become real within our spirit, honest, genuine and burning with the love, fruit and character of our Lord. It is then that we truly began to deal with the lion of our flesh.

We must never allow the works of our flesh—or the works of our hands—to overcome and replace our intimate relationship with Him. We must always have total dependence on Him! Our faith and confidence must always remain in the abilities of His Spirit. I shudder when I hear a minister use the phrase, "I am a self-made man. I have reached down and pulled myself up by my own bootstraps." Remember the fate of King Uzziah.

And he did what was right in the sight of the Lord, according to all that his father Amaziah had done. He sought God in the days of Zechariah, who had understanding in the visions of God; and as long as he sought the Lord, God made him prosper. And he made devices in Jerusalem, invented by skillful men, to be on the towers and the corners, to shoot arrows and large stones. So his fame spread far and wide, for he was marvelously helped till he became strong. But when he was strong his heart was lifted up, **to his destruction**, for he transgressed against the Lord his God by entering the temple of the Lord to burn incense on the altar of incense (II Chronicles 26:4-5,15-16).

All we have and all we are is because of Him!

There are many faiths in this world. The Buddhists have faith, the Hindus have faith, the Muslims fast and pray with faith. None of these faiths results in a closer walk with Jesus. Any experience we receive in the supernatural must result in our drawing closer to Jesus. If a supernatural experience does not increase your faith in God and draw you into a more intimate relationship with Him, avoid it! Every word of faith, operation of a gift and demonstration of the Spirit in signs, wonders and visions should point you to a clearer revelation of the mighty God in Christ. Just because you had a supernatural vision or saw an angel last night does not mean God is dealing with you. We must remember Paul's warning in II Corinthians 11:14-15: "And no wonder! For Satan himself transforms himself into an angel of light. Therefore it is no great thing if his ministers also transform themselves into ministers of righteousness, whose end will be according to their works."

Satan formerly dwelt in the presence of holiness. Ezekiel 28:14 speaks of him: "You were the anointed cherub who covers; I established you; You were on the holy mountain of God; You walked back and forth in the midst of fiery stones." Dwelling in the midst of the fire and glory of God's holiness, he became thoroughly schooled in righteousness.

However, now he has plunged into the depths of wickedness. "...I saw Satan fall like lightning from heaven" (Luke 10:18). The enemy can make evil appear good and good appear evil. He is accomplishing this "magic act" perfectly through the movies that Hollywood produces. In the past fifteen years, every movie that has had any scenes portraying the church, religion or the ministry has portrayed them as rip-off schemes, greedy ministries concerned only with monetary gain, or operations steeped in adultery and power binges. Then they have presented New Age concepts or even atheistic ideas as "pure" and "good" for the institution of the family and for one's spiritual well-being. This is warring against the purity of moral, biblical values in our homes. This destroys our desire for the simplicity of a single-minded loyalty to please and walk in intimacy with Jesus. It puts questions in our minds and destroys the faith our children have in God's vessels. These lions will also destroy the peace, love and simplicity in our homes.

Speaking of the angel that appeared before him, John the Revelator said, "And I fell at his feet to worship him. But he said to me, See that you do not do that! I am your fellow servant, and of your brethren who have the testimony of Jesus. Worship God! For the testimony of Jesus is the spirit of prophecy" (Revelation 19:10). Again I say, if your visions, dreams and supernatural experiences are built upon your faith in angels or some other supernatural phenomenon and not upon God and His Word, you are drastically missing it.

All of our hunger and desire for fasting and praying must not be just to crucify the flesh that we might become greatly anointed or able to see angels and identify demons. We must fast and pray because we are nailing the lion skin of our flesh on the wall of our spiritual house. This is a result of our hunger and desire to walk intimately with Jesus. Then we know that we will make it in the end.

So many people get caught up in the sensationalism of the spirit realm, not realizing that Jesus never intended for us, when walking with Him, to experience that realm exclusively. Yes, there may be occasions that those who love Jesus and are walking with Him will see His heavenly hosts. They can probably identify demonic spirits through discerning of spirits, or have supernatural abilities. Nevertheless, when our walk with God is based on these manifestations and these sensational experiences, they doom us for a fall. Our passion for Jesus will be a conqueror over a thousand evils in our heart. It is the most powerful weapon against the evils that this flesh lusts after.

Often when a person meets the Lord's intimate touch and the heart-changing power of His love, manifestations may result where he may laugh, weep or dance. He may fall out in the spirit or lay prostrate on the floor for hours. We must be certain that these manifestations result from our relationship with God and not from any other source.

During the First Great Awakening, Jonathan Edwards' meetings would often have some of the toughest men falling on the ground and lying prostrate on the floor for up to 24 hours. They got up changed by the power of God. What distorted these revivals the worst were those that got caught up in the manifestations alone, falling out just to fall out, laying just to be seen. Edwards stated that he believed that these men faking the manifestations did more to destroy this revival than the enemies of the revival. We must not get so caught up in a show of demonstration and demand people fall or whatever that we lose what is really important. The main thing is to allow people to draw closer to Jesus and to have their hearts affected and changed by His Word, power and love.

Our human mind is not truly capable of making decisions. It is only capable to carry out what we have already decided in our heart. It is within our heart that we make decisions. When we walk close to Jesus and His Spirit, when His power and love have changed our heart, then we have truly died to the lion of the flesh and the true Lion of the Tribe of Judah can rise in our lives and reign forevermore.

We must set our heart, not just our mind, to seek Him, to seek hard after Him, to truly know Jesus. Acts 4:13 says, "Now when they saw the boldness of Peter and John, and perceived that they were uneducated and untrained men, they marveled. And they realized that they had been with Jesus." You see, a carnal life cannot offer the things that caused these people to stand and take notice of Peter and John. It was not their fleshly wisdom or political influence that caught the people's attention. These two men had made their heart decision to follow Jesus. They had been through their Gethsemane experiences, they had been to the cross, and now here they were walking in the Spirit with Jesus. Because they had that intimate relationship with Him, the world stood up and took notice.

I must emphasize strongly that we desperately need intimacy with Him in this last hour. I have looked at my own life in the past few years and have found occasions in my ministry that

I allowed the lion of the flesh of pride—even my own ego—to rise and give chase to the tinsel dreams of popularity, position and political influence of this world. However, the Lord has been so merciful and has allowed this ministry to experience the times of humble breaking, so that I can see myself as I really am and to see this world for what it really is. It seems, in the six months prior to writing this book, that I have sought to withdraw myself further and further away from the rat race of this political life—the rat race of becoming a "Who's Who" or a "Personality Plus." I would rather have an intimate, fresh, red hot, fiery walk with Jesus than all the shallow, empty masks and walls that so many people live behind.

Jesus said in Matthew 16:6, "Take heed and beware of the leaven of the Pharisees and the Sadducees." Jesus used the example of leaven in natural bread to warn against leaven in the spirit realm, which could be represented as human pride, human ego and a strong willpower. Leaven in bread simply inflates. It does not add substance or nutritional value to the bread. It only puffs it up. When we allow the lions of our flesh to run rampant, they do not add to the life and power of Jesus working inside us. These lions feed on the very part of man that caused the first fall from God's grace and almost every single fall since then. We must become so sick and tired of the lion of our flesh that we will want that intimate, pure, sincere, real walk with Jesus. Such a walk will deal ultimately with these lions.

Jesus is looking for a bride. He is not just looking for someone who dates Him on weekends or who has her own agenda. He is looking for those that will deal with lions of the flesh and walk with Him. In Romans 7:21 Paul said,

I find then a law, that evil is present with me, the one who wills to do good. For I delight in the law of God according to the inward man. But I see another in my members, warring against the law of my mind, and bringing me into the captivity to the law of sin, which is in my members. O, wretched man that I am! Who will deliver me from this body of death?

Paul was so sick and tired of this lion of the flesh that it drove him to that intimate, sacrificial walk with Jesus. Yes, we can only rid ourselves of the lions of our flesh when we are sick and tired of these lions. If we enjoy having the lions around, we will never get rid of them. If we think these lions are just fine, that they will do no harm, we will never rid ourselves of them, nor hang the lion skin on the wall of our spiritual house.

Of course, we must understand that we never actually *kill* the lion of our flesh. There will be occasions where we may feel that the lion skin is hanging on the wall of our spiritual house, only to find the lion rise up at the checkout counter of the grocery store!

This is why Paul wrote in I Corinthians 9:26-27, "Therefore I run thus: not with uncertainty. Thus I fight: not as one who beats the air. But I discipline my body and bring it into subjection, lest, when I have preached to others, I myself should become disqualified."

At any point and time in our lives, no matter how long we have been walking with God, we may allow this lion of our flesh to resurrect itself. It may occur through unconquered flesh or through an undisciplined lifestyle, void of an intimate walk with Jesus. Prayer that becomes just a monotonous time of clocking in and clocking out results in our dreading the moment and being relieved when we are through. We should never be relieved that we are through talking with our Loved One. We should be anxious and longing for more time to spend together in intimate conversation. If we allow this burning love to die, then yes, the lion of our flesh will come alive and seek to destroy the spiritual life within us. This is one reason Paul wrote in Galatians 5:7-9,

> Do not be deceived, God is not mocked; for whatever a man sows, that he will also reap. But he who sows to his flesh will of the flesh reap corruption, but he who sows to the spirit will of the spirit reap everlasting life. Let us not grow weary while doing good, for in due season we shall reap if we do not lose heart.

We must ever seek to walk in the spirit of intimate relationship with Jesus day by day so that we will not fulfill the lust of our flesh and the passion of the lion. When we sense the lion trying to come down off the spiritual wall of our house, then it is again time for that three-day fast to subject ourselves in intimate, focused dedication toward seeking God's face.

In the book of Ruth we find that Naomi left her country of Judah and went to Moab. Originally, Moab was the son of Lot conceived through incest between Lot and his eldest daughter. Moab represents carnality. While in the country of Moab, Naomi and her two daughters-in-law, Orpah and Ruth, experienced the deaths of all three of their husbands. It was not until Naomi had heard how the Lord has visited his people in Judah in giving them bread that she decided to return.

Apostolic revival does not come through making room in our lives for lions to run free. Revival is a direct result of spiritual warfare. When our desire for the ministry of the Word and spiritual things is replaced with carnality, sensationalism and entertainment, a famine is created in us that will drive us to Moab. It will not be until we are sick and tired of the life in Moab that we will begin to hunger again for that intimate relationship with Jesus. The sounds of revival will always draw the hungry. Naomi's decision to spend time satisfying the lions of her flesh in Moab directly affected her children. Lions unchecked in our lives will affect the moral strength of our home! Before we will ever see revival in our city or nation, we must first have revival in our personal lives and homes.

My friend, never allow someone to convince you that establishing a ministry or reaching for a lost soul is more important than your intimate walk with Jesus or your commitment to your family! No amount of success in the ministry or even the saving of a soul is more important than your commitment to walk intimately with God and your commitment to your wife and children. We must remain committed to the spiritual, emotional and physical needs of our family, and that is second only to our consecration to God.

This is why I feel it is important for a young man who is seeking to establish his ministry to exercise the temperance and self-control of the Holy Ghost in waiting to marry until he has sufficiently established his relationship with God and his ministry. By the grace and strength of God, I waited until I was 27 to marry and spent the five-year period between ages 20 and 25 in complete, undistracted devotion to my relationship with God.

When a man finally does choose to marry, his commitment to the ministry does not supersede his family. For those who are married who God has recently called into the ministry or who are wanting a deeper touch of God on their established ministry,

God will give you the grace and strength to accomplish this without neglecting your family. Don't ever give into the feeling that you are being "left behind" or that "your family is an obstacle on the road to establishing a ministry.

My heart is grieved when I see a young man who feels that to be "spiritual," he must be harsh, rejecting and unloving toward his wife. Or one that does not give his family the love, respect and attention they need and deserve. The only thing this proves is that there are lions still running loose in his life. If you will love, cherish and tenderly include your wife and family in your ministry, God will honor you and open all doors for you.

My fellow pastor, evangelist, or prophet, forget about reaching and influencing a city if you first have not established the priority of commitment to your family! Shame on you if you pray for everyone else in the altars, but do not pray for your own kids. Your family's souls are the most important souls in your ministry. I have time and again asked my sweet bride, "Honey, am I feeding you spiritually?" If I am not, no matter how many churches I am spiritually feeding and meeting the needs of, I am a total failure!

The atmosphere of our ministry must not be family unfriendly. All of the "success" in the world concerning our ministries amounts to nothing if our own families do not love and respect us. John Maxwell's definition of success is and excellent one. He quotes, *"true success is discovered when those who are the closest to you love and respect you the most."*

In the past years we have seen some "successful" ministers who have neglected their families to fulfill the "need" for their ministries across the world come crashing to the ground in the flames of adultery and wrecked homes. I have asked myself, "Is it worth it?" No, sir! I have endeavored to set as a standard in our ministry and home life to not be away from my family more than five consecutive days at a time. The only exception is when I travel overseas. I usually give four days to ministering out and three days to my family. A commitment to true family values must remain an unmovable standard in our lives and ministries! Air flight is no longer a status symbol but merely another means of travel. Airfare has become so economical that I can usually fly home for 2-3 days to be with my family when a meeting breaks and goes more than one week. It has been important, though, that my wife and son are in a spiritual church where they can be fed, loved and accepted while I am gone. God has been gracious in allowing us to find this atmosphere at Christian Life Center in Stockton, California.

I have sat on airplanes next to presidents of large corporations, CEO's and successful sales representatives and each has said the same thing: the price he had to pay for this "success" was the loss of his happy family. They are living lives of lonely desperation. They somehow have convinced themselves that they made the right decision. My friend, if I am speaking to you right now, and if you are being tempted to cash your family's stability in for an established ministry among the "big shots," or for power, money or another woman, wake up! You will never make it to the battlefield of Goliath or even of the bear, for these lions will only destroy the things that really matter most.

In Genesis 18:16-20 God shared with His friend Abraham His plans to destroy the wicked cities of Sodom and Gomorrah.

Then the men rose from there and looked toward Sodom, and Abraham went with them to send them on the way. And the Lord said, Shall I hide from Abraham what I am doing, since Abraham shall surely become a great and mighty nation, and all the nations of the earth shall be blessed in him? **For I have known him, in order that he may command his children and his household after him, that they keep the way of the Lord, to do righteousness and justice**, that the Lord may bring to Abraham what He has spoken to him. And the Lord said, "Because the outcry against Sodom and Gomorrah is great, and because their sin is very grave..."

God's confidence was that Abraham could at least reach his family. God in His omniscience knew that Abraham would intercede for the lost souls in Sodom and Gomorrah. God knew He would finally agree to spare the city if ten righteous souls could be found. Among Abraham's family, his nephew Lot, his wife, his sons, daughters and their families, there was the potential of at least ten. If Abraham could have at least affected his family, Sodom and Gomorrah would have been spared.

We may live righteous and godly lives, but if we do not commit ourselves to the spiritual safety of our families, God cannot release us to see victory in further warfares. We profit nothing toward the salvation of this world until we have first committed to the salvation of our families.

When a person becomes content with Moab and allows the lions of sin and carnality to control him, then he will reach a place of self-sufficiency where he will fall prey to the deception that he does not need God. The members of a church congregation may look at their lavish, magnificent building and their established bank accounts and state, "Never again will we have to say, 'Silver and gold have we none,'" but also never again may they say, "In the name of Jesus Christ rise up and walk." **Our total dependency must be upon Jesus.** Paul wrote,

Yet indeed I also count all things loss for the excellence of the knowledge of Christ Jesus my Lord, for whom I have suffered the loss of all things, and count them as rubbish, that I may gain Christ and be found in Him, not having my own righteousness, which is from the law, but that which is through faith in Christ, the righteousness which is from God by faith; **that I may know Him** and the power of His resurrection, and the fellowship of His sufferings, being conformed to His death (Philippians 3:8-10).

We must hunger to know Him. Everything else in Paul's heart—all of his personal attainments—were incidental compared with his desire to know Jesus. We must press on to a deeper relationship with Him.

We can never say that we have arrived or that we have received all of God that we will ever need. Paul lived his life increasing in the spirit of humility. Spiritual maturity will always lead to increased humility. We must not become inflated like the Pharisees. They were so caught up in who they were, in their good works and in their obedience to the do's and don'ts that they could not recognize the Messiah who had come to walk with them and reestablish an intimate relationship with man.

In A.D. 56, Paul declared in his letter to the Galatians that after he visited the original apostles in Jerusalem, they added nothing to him (Galatians 2:6). We find that about six years later, in I Corinthians 15:9, he called himself the least of the apostles. In his letter to the Ephesians, written about A.D. 61, he declared himself to be the least of all saints (Ephesians 3:8). Writing to Timothy in A.D. 65, he declared himself to be the chief of sinners (I Timothy 1:15), adding that God had had mercy on him. The further Paul went in his life and the more intimate he got with Jesus, the less he depended on his own flesh.

He wrote in Philippians 3:3, "For we are the circumcision who worship God in the spirit, rejoice in Christ Jesus, and have no confidence in the flesh." Paul allowed the death of the lion of his flesh to bring him the spiritual understanding and awareness that his total confidence, his total sustenance, his complete strength and ability were in God.

We must reach that place, in prayer, in fasting or in whatever it takes in our relationship with Jesus, where we realize our inabilities and thus become aware of His great abilities and spiritual gifts that He has offered to us.

In II Corinthians Paul spoke of the "death" that he suffered and the reason that he had to go through it. Often we face the same death of the lions of our flesh and we cry out wondering, "What is going on in my life? Why is everything being torn apart?" Yet if we will face ourselves and be honest, we will realize that we grow the least when we have the least resistance. In weightlifting, a person will grow strong muscles from the resistance that he is pressing against. The greater the resistance, the stronger he becomes. So it is in the spirit realm. The greater the resistance, the greater our spiritual man grows as well as our dependence on the supernatural ability of God's spirit. Often when we are praying for a lighter load, we should really be praying for a stronger back! Paul said in II Corinthians 1:8-10,

For we do not want you to be ignorant, brethren, of our trouble which came to us in Asia: that we were burdened beyond measure, about strength, so that we despaired even of life. Yes, we had the sentence of death in ourselves, that we should not trust in ourselves, but in God who raises the dead, who delivered us from so great a death and does deliver us; in whom we trust that he will still deliver us.

In *Strong's Greek and Hebrew Lexicon* this scripture reads, "And asking myself whether I should come out safe from mortal peril, I answered, I must die, that we should not have confidence in ourselves but in God who raises the dead."

When the lion of our flesh has died then God can raise us from that death. We then indeed can have great confidence, not in ourselves, but in the working and operation of God and of His mighty hand.

In John 12:24, Jesus is recorded as saying, "Most assuredly, I say to you, unless a grain of wheat falls into the ground and dies, it remains alone; but if it dies, it produces much fruit." In order to be fruitful and blessed in His kingdom and to do a greater work in the spirit realm, we must first die out and destroy the lion of our flesh. When we choose to defeat this lion and when the lion skin is hanging on the wall of our spiritual house, then and only then can we move into the higher dimensions of authority in our prayers.

Many prematurely attempt to jump onto the battlefield of Goliath, saying, "I am going to take this giant down." We then read of their failures in the newspapers or hear about them in the media, not because God or His power has failed, but because they never dealt with the lions that were in their life in the first place. Before we enter the battlefield of Goliath, we must first face and deal with our lions through our passion and intimate desire to serve God.

In this last hour, many people have found themselves following individuals who have been good administrators, promoters or theologians rich with the wisdom of this world, but who, sadly, have never discovered an intimate relationship with God that results from an incredible hunger to know Him. We must never turn Christianity into a history lesson. **It must be always a fervent love affair.**

A.D. Urshan, that great man of God who lived earlier in this century, once stated, "Seek not the glory of God, seek His face. Seek not His blessings, seek the cross. Seek not honor, but seek humility." Oh, what great truth there is in those words. When we have truly made Jesus **our everything**, when He becomes our sustenance, when He becomes our strength, when He becomes everything to us, then and only then can He be glorified in us and through us.

Thomas A. Kempis once said,

When we set ourselves in the lowest place, the highest place will be given to us, for the highest cannot stand without the lowest. The chiefest saints before God are the least before themselves and the more glorious they are so much within themselves are they more humble.

One of the most beautiful things that God has allowed our ministry to experience was when we were invited to be a part of the intercessory prayer team that traveled to Ethiopia with Billy Cole in March 1994. Each year a crusade is held in a primitive village called Wara. It is here that more than 200,000 believers gather with one thing on their mind: to worship Jesus and lift Him up. The thing that broke me the most was the humility and the total dependence these brethren have toward God. They have nothing, but really have everything because they have

JOHN ARCOVIO

learned to **be rich in faith—the most wealthy possession a man could ever have in this life**.

When our bus pulled up to the crusade for the first night, those precious Ethiopian brethren—many of whom have suffered greatly for the name of Jesus, *spending more time in jail than out of jail* for preaching the gospel—were joyfully welcoming us. Many carried scars on their backs from being beaten for preaching this precious gospel. When I looked out and saw them leaping in the air with their hands lifted, worshiping and praising God with such joyous fervency, I began to weep uncontrollably. As we stepped out and began to walk toward the crusade area, they came and fell on their faces, reaching out to touch the men of God. **Not because we were Americans, oh, no! Not because we were white! (Shame on anyone who would have such an egotistical, puffed-up mind set.)** Their leader, Brother Teklemariam, had taught them that the highest honor in the world was to be touched by a man of God and to be blessed by him. When I saw these precious brethren doing this, I was so broken. When one Ethiopian brother, who was so much more broken, so much more committed than I could ever dream to be, fell to his knees near me to be blessed, I fell down with him. As comical as this may sound, we both fell down until we were flat on our faces before God. I wept and said to these brethren, "No, lay hands upon me, for I need to be blessed by you." **I ask you, could we in America finally lower ourselves to the point that God can lift us up?** If we will, then we will begin to see true apostolic revival burn in our midst.

Human intellect, resources, wisdom, willpower, and political influence are all totally inadequate. We do not need more resources in America to accomplish the will of God. What we need is to go back to the **only source** and that is Jesus. **For all**

too long in America, we have given honor and prestige to things that mean nothing in the sight of God. We honor the evangelist who can flip his schedule book open and brag about being booked for two years in advance, and we shun the humble, contrite, broken evangelists who are waiting upon God with open schedules, truly seeking His face for direction. They are not for hire, not interested in just filling schedules and "staying busy." **It is time for the church in America to humble herself and repent!** America has honored the pastors who are carnal, self-seeking, political, and who push their own ambitions and kingdoms. Paul, while weeping, wrote of these in Philippians 3:19, saying, "They glory in their shame."

The Lord spoke to Samuel and said, "Do not look at his appearance, or at the height of his stature, because I have refused him, for the Lord does not see as man sees; for man looks at the outward appearance, but the Lord looks at the heart" (I Samuel 16:7). All too often we are swept away by political trappings and "look at the outward appearance"; it is by this that the American church has been entangled for so many years. We must seek the ways that please God! **It is time for the sons and daughters of God to stand and allow God to bring the pure, unadulterated motive of His Spirit in our midst!**

It is a sad day when the church becomes more excited about voting for a candidate, to place him in office as a "Christian" than they do about seeking the face of God. It is a sad day when a church puts more faith in a political party than in praying and touching the throne of God. **The church must never give more time, effort and resources to politics than to spreading the gospel.** We may gain all the political influence in this world and not accomplish a fraction as much as we would if we had true influence with God.

What is happening to our nation in this hour is not because we did not vote, it is because we will not pray. We enjoy the lions of our flesh running around. We have enjoyed them and we see nothing wrong with them. It is time for the lion skins to be hung on the walls of our house.

In the book of Acts, the world simply recognized Peter and John as having been with Jesus. The leaders of their day did not **vote** for them, but they did take **note** of them, not because of their education, nor because of their training, nor because of anything the lions of their flesh had to offer. They took note of them simply because they had spent time with Jesus.

When we come out of our closets of prayer charged with His spirit and power, the world will stand up and pay attention. Simple faith moves God, looses His angels and releases His gifts and can accomplish more than all the political maneuvering, wealth and influence this world could ever offer. This may sound trite, nevertheless it is true!

It is truly time for us to destroy the lions of our flesh so that we may move into a greater dimension of authority in the battle, that of warfare with the bear! When you leave the lion of your flesh hanging on the wall, then the prayers that you prayed for so many years take on a new authority, a new dimension of power. This is the dimension of the warfare of the bear.

2

THE BEAR:
WARFARE OF THE SPIRITUAL
STRONGHOLD IN YOUR CITY

David had been keeping his father's sheep for many years now and was proud of his spotless record. Not one sheep—even down to the smallest lamb—had been lost. His reputation for being a prudent and valiant young man whom the Lord favored had spread throughout the country. Even when a ferocious bear had attacked the sheep in the middle of the night, the Lord delivered the bear into David's hand. Hanging on the wall of his room back home were the skins of both a lion and a bear, giving testimony to the delivering hand of Jehovah God of Israel that rested upon David.

One day word reached the elders of the humble town of Bethlehem that the prophet Samuel had come to visit. Because of their king's backslidden state, most of the nation had fallen into apostasy. Was this visit one of judgment and doom? History had taught the people to fear the word of God's true prophets.

Trembling, the elders approached Samuel and said, "Do you come peaceably?" Samuel replied, "Peaceably; I have come to sacrifice to the Lord. Sanctify yourselves, and come with me to the sacrifice." Then Samuel did a great honor unto Jesse's household by calling for Jesse and his sons to be sanctified for the sacrifice also. No one even thought to send for David, for he was out tending the sheep. Besides, he was the youngest and smallest of all the brothers.

After all seven sons had passed before Samuel, and though each was impressive from his countenance and stature, the Lord still had not moved upon the prophet to anoint any of them the next king of Israel. Samuel was puzzled—surely God's perfect number was seven, and God had never given a kingdom to one beyond the seventh child. Then Samuel asked, "Are all the young men here?" Jesse replied, "There remains yet the youngest, and there he is, keeping the sheep." Samuel said, "Send and bring him. For we will not sit down till he comes here."

When David entered the room, he did not seem like king material to the natural eye. Perhaps someday he would make a good shepherd, reasoned all present, for all he seemed to care about was taking care of those dumb sheep. Why, he almost gave his life on two separate occasions to save one lamb! Yet the moment he walked into the room, God's anointing fell upon Samuel like a mighty waterfall, and the Word of the Lord was spoken: "Arise, anoint him; for this is the one!" Samuel took the horn of oil and poured it upon David's head. As the oil dripped down David's face onto his clothes, the Spirit of the Lord encompassed him like a cloud of glory.

From that day forward David knew he would never be the same. Little did he realize that as God's favor and glory descended upon him, the Spirit of the Lord was departing from Saul, and an evil spirit was taking its place. David's long dark night was just beginning. In the days following, God's will would place him in the royal court to minister to a king that would later seek to destroy his life in a jealous rage.

When David faced the lion, that battle was a victory for himself. Either he was going to kill the lion or the lion was going to kill him. When he faced the bear, it not only was a personal victory, but a victory for his flock. So it is when we face the bear of our life.

When we destroy the lion of our flesh and hang the spiritual lion skin on the wall, this becomes a victory for *us*. The dimension of the bear, however, is the second dimension of warfare that Paul spoke about in Ephesians 6:12: "For we do not wrestle against flesh and blood...*but against powers....*" *Powers* is translated from *exousia* (ex-oo-see'-ah), meaning "supernatural ability or freedom in government." As we move into this second dimension of the bear, we find that we are now dealing with the spiritual strongholds of our particular city.

A church body, which together has fasted, prayed and found that intimate place of walking with Jesus and has dealt with the lions of their lives, will move into the dimension of the warfare of the bear. (A small percentage may still become entangled with the cares of this life and ensnared by the lusts and passions of their souls. Nevertheless, we are speaking of the "core group.") When we have truly conquered and mastered the lions, then God will bring us into a dimension of not just affecting ourselves, but reaching out, affecting and shaking the very foundation of the city in which we live.

This warfare of the bear is a dimension of great spiritual proportions. Saints' prayers that once accomplished nothing suddenly take on new authority and life in the dimension of the bear. Prayers that they once prayed in faith believing but with little or no result suddenly take on new authority! When a church moves into the warfare of the bear, they will shake the heavens. Spiritual strongholds will come crashing down as the god of this world will no longer be able to hide the gospel of the death, burial, and resurrection of our Lord Jesus Christ from the lost. Truly, the burden for the lost souls of the city, as well as late-night travailing and weeping for them, are welcome in the dimension of the bear.

I recall times in my own ministry when I prayed with faith believing for miracles to happen, such as for a lame man to walk out of his wheelchair. Often nothing happened. Then suddenly one day, I prayed the same prayer of faith and it happened. The prayer of faith that I prayed was nothing different. The gifts exercised were no greater. What changed was the dimension I was in. I had moved into the dimension of the bear. Timing is everything in the Kingdom of God. When it is time, God wants us to step forth to believe and these things will take place.

Notice again that *powers* means "supernatural ability or freedom in government." We can see the operation of the "powers of authorities" in our political arena today. Often the most corrupt political bodies are legislatures that allow themselves to become human spirit-led or even worse, demonically inspired.

We find strong scriptural evidence in Acts 12 that supports this truth. It was there that Herod the king stretched out his hand to harass some from the church. Then he went so far as to kill James with his sword. Herod had no personal reason to do this. **Powers of authorities drove him**. This was completely a political move because he saw that it pleased the Jews. Herod had long tried to bring the Jews under his iron fist. Still, they rose against him and resisted him. Now he saw that through political means he could please the Jews and through deceit and destruction he could bring them under his authority. Therefore, he went on to take Peter during the days of the feast of unleavened bread. (This is the Passover—Israel's commemoration of their deliverance from the death angel.)

The church in the book of Acts had dealt with their lions back when God had slain Ananias and Sapphira, causing His fear to fall upon the church. Now they were worshiping God in one accord. The church had entered the battleground of the bear and was about to discover that God had given them authority over this dimension.

When Herod took Peter and threw him into a jail cell surrounded by four squads of soldiers, the church did not go and demand their rights. Nor did they sign petitions or gather around the jail house and march with signs in protest to what was happening to the rights of their fellow believer. What the church did was spend one night in prayer, seeking the face of God on Peter's behalf. Because they had entered the battlefield of the bear, this all-night prayer meeting resulted in the breaking of the back of the bear. Acts 12:6-9 says,

> When Herod was about to bring him out that night, Peter was sleeping, bound with two chains between two soldiers; and the guards before the door were keeping the prison. Now behold, an angel of the Lord stood by him, and a light shone in the prison; and he struck Peter on the side and raised him up, saying, "Arise, quickly!" And his chains fell

off his hands. Then the angel said to him, "Gird yourself and tie on your sandals"; and so he did. And he said to him, "Put on your garment and follow me." So, he went out and followed him and did not know that what was done by the angel was real, but thought he was seeing a vision.

This all-night prayer meeting loosed the angel of God to minister on behalf of the heirs of salvation. All it took was one all-night prayer meeting from a church that had already defeated the lions of their flesh.

I believe the answer this hour is not to increase the Christian vote in America or to put Christians in leadership. Even if every seat in Congress were filled with Holy-Ghost-filled Christians, I do not believe that they would necessarily turn evil back. Faithful, humble saints who will dare to pray and persistently fast will see the yokes of evil destroyed by the hand of God. We must start dealing with the lions of the flesh and go for the bears of our city. A Spirit-led church that deals with their lions through fasting and prayer can turn the weapons of the enemy back upon the enemy. This church will not back down in the heat of persecution when they arouse the bear of their city.

In your city, if powers of authorities have caused men in positions of influence and power to rise against your church, do not panic, for this may be a sign that your church has entered the battlefield of the bear. Apostolic revival comes not when the Spirit has stirred the church, but when a city becomes stirred.

When only the church board rises against us, we have not yet seen the warfare of the bear, for we are still dealing with lions of the flesh in the church. It is when the church has found that intimate place of subjection to Jesus, walking in humility and unity with each other, that the true warfare with the bear commences.

You may ask, "How will we know when we have entered the dimension of the warfare of the bear? How will we know when we have crossed the point of authority in our prayers that separate the dimension of the lion from the dimension of the bear?" My friend, nobody has to tell you when you rouse a bear. You know what has happened when a bear rises out of its hibernation and comes clawing at you.

So many of our American cities have bears, or powers of authorities, that laid hibernating, untouched for hundreds of years. Thank God for churches who now through prayer and fasting are reaching into untouched cities for souls. Through this apostolic authority, they are beginning to stir the bear out of his long winter sleep. You will know, my friend, when you have stirred up the powers of authorities in your city. The mayor of your city may fight your church. School principals and teachers may persecute your children. The city council may refuse permits to build—you may suffer all kinds of attacks. Recognize the spirit behind the people. You have come up against the bear, the battleground of powers of authorities.

I believe when a person or a church goes on a seven-to-ten-day fast that they move into the dimension of the warfare of the bear, and their focus moves beyond themselves and into pouring themselves out for the sake of souls.

Two of the highest honors in life are to be an **interceding prayer warrior** and a **soul winner**. In I Corinthians 10:33 Paul said, "Just as I also please all men in all things, not seeking my own profit, but the profit of many, that they may be saved."

When the church moves into the dimension of the bear through prayer and fasting, they focus upon the purpose of

God. That purpose extends all the way back to the reason why He even created man: to have man to serve Him. God's purpose in this hour is not to build earthly kingdoms. In John 18:36 Jesus answered, "My kingdom is not of this world. If My kingdom were of this world, My servants would fight, so that I should not be delivered to the Jews; but now My kingdom is not from here." God's purpose is not necessarily to heal the sick, raise the dead or cleanse the lepers. God's purpose in this hour is to redeem lost mankind unto Himself. Luke 19:10 says, "For the Son of Man has come to seek and to save that which was lost."

I believe the two strongest weapons in the warfare of the bear are **prayer and fasting.** For many years the Apostolic Church of Ethiopia has designated every Friday night as an all-night prayer meeting. When I returned from the Ethiopian crusade in 1994, I immediately endeavored to hold an all-night prayer meeting in every week of revival. As a result, my physical health hit a brick wall in November 1994 and for 1½ months I was unable to effectively pray or even fast one day. Too much of any one thing is not good. The Lord impressed upon me that if I would seek His face in the consistency and moderation of an hour or so per day with one or two all-night prayer meetings per month and live daily in "the Spirit of prayer," He would honor it greatly!

What I believe God meant by "the Spirit of prayer" was communing with Him every day in our spirits, on the highway, in the grocery store, at the mall, at work, at school—living daily in the spirit of prayer. This coupled with our consistent "hour of prayer" will bring apostolic results in the warfare of the bear, fighting for our cities.

Psalm 65:4 says, "Blessed is the man You choose, And cause to approach You, that he may dwell in Your courts. We shall be satisfied with the goodness of Your house, of Your holy temple." Yes, being a prayer warrior is one of the highest honors in life. It is on your face in prayer that you gain influence with God. Others may scoff and mock you but when you choose to spend time alone with God in prayer and fasting, you equip yourself in the greatest manner possible for the battle.

Exodus 33:11 says, "So the Lord spoke to Moses face to face, as a man speaks to his friend. And he would return to the camp, but his servant Joshua the son of Nun, a young man, did not depart from the tabernacle." This young man Joshua, who chose to spend his time alone in the tabernacle seeking the face of God, later emerged as a powerful figure in Israel. Joshua was not trying to rub shoulders with the "Who's Who" of his day or climb any ladders of man's influence. He chose to seek the influence of the One who could help him the most. We read later in Joshua 10:8-14,

And the Lord said to Joshua, "Do not fear them, for I have delivered them into your hand; not a man of them shall stand before you." Joshua therefore came upon them suddenly, having marched all night from Gilgal. So the Lord routed them before Israel, killed them with a great slaughter at Gibeon, chased them along the road that goes to Beth Horon, and struck them down as far as Azekah and Makkedah. And it happened, as they fled before Israel and were on the descent of Beth Horon, that the Lord cast down large hailstones from heaven on them as far as Azekah, and they died. There were more who died from the hailstones than the children of Israel killed with the sword. Then Joshua spoke to the Lord in the day when the Lord delivered up the Amorites before the children of Israel, and he said in the sight of Israel: "Sun, stand still over Gibeon; and Moon, in the Valley of Aijalon." So the sun stood still, and the moon stopped, till the people had revenge upon their enemies. Is this not written in the Book of Jasher? So the sun stood still in the midst of heaven, and did not hasten to go down for about a whole day. And there has been no day like that, before it or after it, that the Lord heeded the voice of a man; for the Lord fought for Israel.

This young man prays one word of faith and the God of glory stops the universe for him. Now that's influence with God! God has chosen to operate through the principles of prayer and fasting. Job 36:26-29 says,

Behold, God is great, and we do not know Him; nor can the number of His years be discovered. For He draws up drops of water, which distill as rain from the mist, which the clouds drop down and pour abundantly on man. Indeed, can anyone understand the spreading of clouds, the thunder from His canopy?

The amount of "spiritual mist" we send up through prayer and fasting is reflected in the "spiritual rain" God sends down from heaven. Many churches experience "spiritual droughts" because they lay aside the weapons of prayer and fasting even in the midst of the warfare of the bear. The excuse often is, "I am so busy with revival and the demands of the work of God that I really do not have time to pray." No spiritual mists through prayer and fasting going up, no heavenly outpourings of spiritual rain. Jacob, in Genesis 28:16-22, "met" God at Bethel, which means "the house of God."

> Then Jacob awoke from his sleep and said, "Surely the Lord is in this place, and I did not know it." And he was afraid and said, "How awesome is this place! This is none other than the house of God, and this is the gate of heaven!" Then Jacob rose early in the morning, and took the stone that he had put at his head, set it up as a pillar, and poured oil on top of it. And he called the name of that place Bethel; but the name of that city had been Luz previously. Then Jacob made a vow, saying, "If God will be with me, and keep me in this way that I am going, and give me bread to eat and clothing to put on, so that I come back to my father's house in peace, then the Lord shall be my God. And this stone which I have set as a pillar shall be God's house, and of all that You give me I will surely give a tenth to You."

It was not until Peniel in Genesis 32:25-30 that his life became changed forever!

> Then Jacob was left alone; and a Man wrestled with him until the breaking of day. Now when He saw that He did not prevail against him, He touched the socket of his hip; and the socket of Jacob's hip was out of joint as He wrestled with him. And He said, "Let Me go, for the day breaks." But he said, "I will not let You go unless You bless me!" So He said to him, "What is your name?" He said, "Jacob." And He said, "Your name shall no longer be called Jacob, but Israel; for you have struggled with God and with men, and have prevailed." Then Jacob asked, saying, "Tell me

Your name, I pray." And He said, "Why is it that you ask about My name?" And He blessed him there. And Jacob called the name of the place Peniel: "For I have seen God face to face, and my life is preserved."

We can go to a church, sit on a pew and "meet" God there, but it will not be until our Peniel experience of seeking the face of God through times of prayer and fasting that we will truly become changed. One all-night prayer meeting can change the course of history, as it did with Jacob.

Esau was coming to meet Jacob to seek revenge for Jacob's past injustice when Jacob chose to wrestle all night with the angel of the Lord. For 32 years Esau had seethed in bitterness, plotting his revenge against his brother, but all it took was one all-night prayer meeting to change the heart of a man who had been bitter for 32 years.

My friend, it does not matter how long you may have been facing your impossible situation. You may be on the verge of a tremendous miracle and all it may take is one all-night session of seeking the face of God to change your situation! We need gladiators of the Spirit realm to rise in this hour, mighty in prayer, to affect warfare against the bears of spiritual darkness in our city. Who will dare to gain influence with God through prayer in this midnight hour?

I Samuel 1:9-20 says,

So Hannah arose after they had finished eating and drinking in Shiloh. Now Eli the priest was sitting on the seat by the doorpost of the tabernacle of the Lord. And she was in bitterness of soul, and prayed to the Lord and wept in anguish. Then she made a vow and said, "O Lord of hosts, if You will indeed look on the affliction of Your maidservant and remember me, and not forget Your maidservant, but will give Your maidservant a male child, then I will give him to the Lord all the days of his life, and no razor shall come upon his head." And it happened, as she continued praying before the Lord, that Eli watched her mouth. Now Hannah spoke in her heart; only her lips moved, but her voice was not heard. Therefore Eli thought she was drunk. So Eli said to her, "How long will you be drunk? Put your wine away from you!" And Hannah answered and said, "No, my lord, I am a woman of sorrowful spirit. I have drunk neither wine nor intoxicating drink, **but have poured out my soul before the Lord.** Do not consider your maidservant a wicked woman, for out of the abundance of my complaint and grief I have spoken until now." Then Eli answered and said, "Go in peace, and the God of Israel grant your petition which you have asked of Him." And she said, "Let your maidservant find favor in your sight." So the woman went her way and ate, and her face was no longer sad. Then they rose early in the morning and worshiped before the Lord, and returned and came to their house at Ramah. And Elkanah knew Hannah his wife, and the Lord remembered her. So it came to pass in the process of time that Hannah conceived and bore a son, and called his name Samuel, saying, "Because I have asked for him from the Lord."

When verse 15 says, **"but have poured out my soul before the Lord,"** it literally means Hannah "multiplied her prayers before God." The resulting product of this godly woman's prayers was Samuel, the mighty intercessor and Man of God.

When we choose to **"pray in the Spirit"** through tongues or travailing, our prayers become multiplied before God. We are so limited when we choose to pray only in the English language. We may only be able to cover twenty or thirty requests in an hour's time, or as many as our mind can remember. When we choose to **pray in the Spirit**, the Spirit can cover thousands of requests in a short time.

I have been in all-night prayer meetings where the Spirit revealed that some dear sister travailing in the corner was interceding for nations! Because of the power of this revelation, I now spend 75-80% of my prayer time praying in the Spirit. I have found that all-night prayer meetings seem to go by quicker and I do not find myself facing "dead spots" searching for things to pray about or mundanely repeating, "Ooooohhh God." When we **pray in the Spirit**, we are also assured that we are praying according to the will of God!

Romans 8:26-27 supports all that I just stated.

Likewise the Spirit also helps in our weaknesses. For we do not know what we should pray for as we ought, but the Spirit Himself makes intercession for us with **groanings which cannot be uttered**. Now He who searches the hearts knows what the **mind of the Spirit is**, because He makes intercession for the saints **according to the will of God**.

I challenge you to begin to spend the majority of your time **praying in the Spirit**, and watch if you do not start experiencing apostolic results like never before!

Brother Teklemariam shared with me a true story that took place in Ethiopia in about 1990. Due to the strong stand for the name of Jesus by the Apostolic Church of Ethiopia, severe persecution from witch doctors, the Coptic (Ethiopian Orthodox) Church, socialists, communists, Muslims, and Trinitarian denominations rose against them.

In a certain village was a Seventh-Day Adventist church that had been in existence for about fourteen years. It had never made any significant spiritual accomplishments, save for a few humanitarian efforts through the bringing in of food and medical supplies.

In that church was an Adventist preacher who, though he was a preacher, had not been delivered from the idols he still worshiped. Because of this he had lost his mind.

One day while reading Acts 2, he saw the revelation of Jesus' name baptism and the mighty God in Christ. When God opened his eyes to the revelation, he returned to his right mind. He went to the Adventist church and asked to be baptized in Jesus' name. They refused.

He searched all over for a church to baptize him in Jesus' name but found none. One day a young person from the Apostolic Church of Ethiopia came to his village and witnessed to him about one-God, Jesus' name baptism. This young preacher was then baptized in the wonderful name of Jesus and he received the Holy Ghost in a mighty experience in Brother Teklemariam's office.

He went back to his village preaching Jesus' name. The men from the Adventist church began to fight him. They locked him in prison and put his son in a vessel of boiling water, burning him badly, thinking the man would return to the Adventist church. Nevertheless, he continued preaching the truth of one-God, Jesus' name baptism. Then the men took all of his cows and locked them in a barn with no food or water, eventually killing them.

JOHN ARCOVIO

You see, in spite of an Adventist church being in this village, demonic control completely bound the area.

A witch doctor held the village in a grip of fear. He controlled the people through demonic spirits. These spirits possessed a python living in a big clump of trees above the village. This python, which was about 35 feet long, was filled with thousands of devils just as the pigs in the New Testament were filled with legions of devils. Often, during the night, a whirling wind would descend upon the village and pick up the children and feed them to the python. The village was bound by fear and they had sought deliverance through the witch doctor, piling large amounts of money and gifts at his feet. The witch doctor would offer up sacrifices and for a little while the python spirits would be appeased. Soon though, the demons would rise up and come back into the village and the scenario would be repeated. The witch doctor learned that through manipulation of the spirits he could control the village. This went on year after year after year.

During prayer one day the converted Adventist preacher opened his Bible to Isaiah 57. As he was reading, the Spirit of the Lord came upon him and illuminated verse 13, "When you cry out, let your collection of idols deliver you. But the wind will carry them all away, a breath will take them, **but he who puts his trust in me shall possess the land, and shall inherit my holy mountain."**

He stood up and went to some brethren and shared this word of faith. He then decided to go on a three-day fast with his brethren. The man then stepped out by faith and walked up to the grove of trees and said within himself, "This mountain, this hill of trees does not belong to the demons of this python, nor to the demons of this witch doctor. This belongs to God." He then cried with a loud voice and said, "Demons of the pythons, demons of the grove of trees, I command you in the name of Jesus to leave this place." When this was spoken, many of the village people gathered around and began to laugh and mock him for his seemingly absurd boldness.

Suddenly, the demons of the python rose up in the air above the trees and cried out with a loud voice, "People of the village, listen to me. This Apostolic preacher, the doctrine that he preaches has taken my authority away. I can no longer stay here. I must go." With a rush the thousands of demons left the python and a mighty wind carried the python away, never to be seen again. When the people saw this, they came running and fell down upon their knees, lifting their hands toward heaven and saying, "If your God can do this, we want to serve the God you serve." Many people were baptized in Jesus' name and were filled with the Holy Ghost.

After the python left, the Apostolic preacher cut down the grove of trees. The government then donated a parcel of land and the Apostolic Church began to build an building for the glory of Jesus' name.

The church of Ethiopia has dealt with the lion in their own personal lives and has begun to see the bears of each city destroyed, their backs having been broken. Brother Teklemariam has stated that God has reaped a mighty harvest from fields that the church did not sow seeds in. The thousands and thousands of people that had come up in Trinitarian, Baptist, Lutheran, Assembly of God, Catholic, and Coptic churches were receiving the revelation of the Oneness message. Thousands are being added to the Apostolic Church of Ethiopia daily.

Trinitarian leaders have come to Brother Teklemariam, wanting to join hands with him in revival, but have turned back when they have seen the strong stand for the one-God, Jesus' name message that the Apostolic Church has taken. This has been to their hurt, for the people, who are so hungry for truth and the whole counsel of God, have been steadily coming to be filled with the Holy Ghost and baptized in Jesus' name. Persecution has come from these churches, but the Apostolic Church has not backed down or compromised the message. God has stood for His people, and the fear of God is spreading among all those who have fought the message.

We have the most precious revelation in this hour. We must preserve it! People are hungry for truth. We need to pray that God will bring to all churches, from the largest to the smallest, the revelation of this precious message of the death (repentance), burial (baptism in Jesus' name) and resurrection (receiving the Holy Spirit). If the churches will not receive it but will instead fight against this message, then we need to pray God will begin harvesting the people.

That wonderful message is contained in Acts 2:38: "Then Peter said to them, 'Repent, and let every one of you be baptized in the name of Jesus Christ for the remission of sins; and you shall receive the gift of the Holy Spirit.'"

Repentance is asking God to forgive you for your sins and determining to turn your back on sin. II Corinthians 7:10 says, "For godly sorrow produces repentance leading to salvation, not to be regretted; but the sorrow of the world produces death."

Baptism is by immersion in water in Jesus' name to put off the old man and to put on Christ. Galatians 3:27 says, "For as many of you as were baptized into Christ have put on Christ." Romans 6:5-6 teaches,

For if we have been united together in the likeness of His death, certainly we also shall be in the likeness of His resurrection, knowing this, that our old man was crucified with Him, that the body of sin might be done away with, that we should no longer be slaves of sin.

When we put on Christ through water baptism in Jesus' name, that old sinful garment we used to live in is removed and we put on the purity of the robes of righteousness—God's righteousness. Isaiah 64:6-9 says,

But we are all like an unclean thing, and all our righteousnesses are like filthy rags; we all fade as a leaf, and our iniquities, like the wind, have taken us away. And there is no one who calls on Your name, who stirs himself up to take hold of You; for You have hidden Your face from us, and have consumed us because of our iniquities. But now, O Lord, You are our Father; we are the clay, and You our potter; and all we are the work of Your hand. Do not be furious, O Lord, nor remember iniquity forever; Indeed, please look—we all are Your people!

Receiving the Holy Spirit is evidenced by speaking in an unknown tongue. Acts 2:4 says, "And they were all filled with the Holy Spirit and began to speak with other tongues, as the Spirit gave them utterance." "For they heard them speak with tongues and magnify God" (Acts 10:46).

No, my friend, this precious message is not hindering the growth of our churches. What hinders the growth of our churches is that we are not willing to deal with the lions of our flesh, and face the challenges of the bear and the giant.

For example, five years ago the headquarters church in Addis Ababa, Ethiopia, had an attendance of approximately 200 people. This same church, which has dealt with their lions and has not only moved into the dimension of warfare of the bear but has seen the back of the bear of their city broken, now runs in excess of 5,000 people. They have had all-night prayer meetings every Friday night for more than fifteen years. Twice a year they call every member of the church on a seven-day fast. All this is not done for greater anointing or greater power; it is done in humility, hunger and desire to draw closer to Jesus. These apostolic principles have produced a humble, broken and contrite people who have one passion: loving Jesus and winning souls for Him.

Paul wrote of this single-minded affection in Philippians 3:7-8: "But what things were gain to me, these I have counted loss for Christ. Yet indeed I also count all things loss for the excellence of the knowledge of Christ Jesus my Lord, for whom I have suffered the loss of all things, and count them as rubbish, that I may gain Christ."

If we will preserve our love for Jesus and our desire to win souls, we will succeed. It is does not matter what country you are in. It does not matter if you are in Asia, Africa, Europe, Australia or the Americas. God's principles do work. Anointing, faith and the demonstration of God's Spirit and power are not prejudiced. They will operate in any heart regardless of nationality, color or creed. All God is looking for are hungry and willing hearts.

America will experience this land-shaking revival. We are standing on the brink of the greatest revival since the book of Acts. This is our hour! This is our time! If we will dare to face the challenge of the bears of our city, if we will dare to see the backs of these bears broken, then we will see a "book of Acts" move of God here in America. This is our hour! Now is the time! We must preach this message everywhere.

When you rouse up the bear in your city through prayer and fasting, you will suffer persecution. The witch doctor in the Ethiopian village where all the people had been converted after the python was destroyed grew furious. He was forced to admit that the power he had when the demons were in the python was now gone.

One day, while some of the brethren were building the Apostolic church out of the wood cut from the grove of trees, this witch doctor ordered his servant to shoot them with a machine gun. This servant stood about forty yards away, pointed the machine gun in their direction and emptied it. Miraculously, not even one of the bullets touched the brethren.

The brethren gathered all the spent shells from the bullets and showed them to a government official. Subsequently, the officials came and arrested the witch doctor and his servant. Then the officials stood in front of the whole village with a loud proclamation: "Hear us, people of the village. The Apostolic Church of Ethiopia now has authority to worship in this area. If you have any problem with them, come to us, because if you touch them again you will have us to reckon with."

This is truly what happens when a church dares to ignore the pressures and persecution that may come from entering into the warfare of the bear.

Brother Teklemariam shared with me many stories of how Trinitarian pastors have come and set Apostolic churches on fire and how God's judgments have fallen upon them. God's hand protects His true church!

In one village a community leader burned a church down. The next day the brethren stood on the ashes, lifted their hands, praised God and stated loudly to the people, "We will build yet again another church in the same place." After the second church was built, the community leader burned it down as well. Soon fire from heaven fell upon him. He burned for five days before dying. After he died, the people laid soaking wet blankets upon him to cool him down, yet steam rose up from them. Finally they had to wrap him with banana leaves and carry him on branches in order to bury him.

As a result of this one leader's persecution and death, more than 68,000 people have been baptized in Jesus' name in this area.

In another instance, a Lutheran pastor in a jealous rage took his machine gun and shot seventy bullets into an Apostolic pastor's house. Not one person, not even an animal, was hurt. The next day lightning fell from heaven and struck the attacker. He fell to the ground burning from an invisible fire. For an entire day electricity ran up and down his body until he died. When the people tried to pick his body up, they were unable to because of the electrical charge on him. They had to get shock-resistant tools to pick him up to bury him. From that moment on, all across Ethiopia, the fear of God fell upon all the Trinitarians that fought the Apostolic Church. It was said everywhere that, "The God of the Oneness Apostolic Church kills all who resist and fight them. Don't persecute or touch them."

This is the result of a church daring to war with the bear, or the powers of the authorities of their city.

Perhaps you are an evangelist reading this book right now and wondering, "Where do I fit in? Where does my ministry fit in?" If you will fast, pray and dare to deal the lion of your flesh,

God will give you the authority to step into each and every city He leads you to. You will be able to lead that particular church into the dimension of warfare of the bear.

Perhaps you are a pastor and the sheep you are leading are satisfied and willing to leave the lions of their lives as they are. If you will by faith simply lead the way in the warfare of the lion, you will have a core group that will respond. God will use those faithful few and help bring a breakthrough in your city.

Perhaps you have been up against a spiritual wall in your city for many years and feel as though it will never break. You may feel that you have tried everything. You have fasted and you have prayed in all-night prayer meetings. Allow me to share with you a spiritual principle which I believe pertains to your situation. Some spirits are like schoolyard bullies who try to push you around. If you let them push you around, they will push you around for the rest of your life. But if you ever step out and say, "Boo," they are gone. All they need is for you to call their bluff.

Then again you may be up against other spirits which that do not run when you say, "Boo." Nothing seems to change when you go on that ten-day fast. They do not step aside and give way to revival. The back of this supernatural force is not broken, even when your church moves into a series of all-night prayer meetings.

In this second dimension of the warfare of the bear, the spiritual strongholds are like pesky flies. Our Lord Himself referred to the devil as Beelzebub, the lord of the flies. In Matthew 10:25 He said, "It is enough for a disciple that he be like his teacher, and a servant like his master. If they have called the master of the house Beelzebub, how much more will they call those of his household!"

Pesky flies are persistent. They persevere. A fly, when you swat at it, does not leave you alone. It comes back again and again and again. However, it is amazing that, among certain species, a fly's life span is only 72 hours. Therefore though they fight fierce and fight hard, they are not in it for the long run. They are only short-term fighters. Persistent and pesky notwithstanding, they cannot hang on for the full fight.

My dear faithful pastor, you will outlast those pesky flies by simply continuing to do what you know is right. Continue to deal with the lions of the flesh. Refuse to open the door of your church and allowing them to roam free. Continue to hold on by faith with prayer and fasting. **You will outlast those pesky flies.**

The battle is not ours—it is the Lord's. He is the ultimate spiritual pest exterminator!

Let us move on now and look into the next and final dimension of warfare that stands between us and apostolic revival: the warfare of Goliath, or that of the giant of our nation.

3

GOLIATH: WARFARE OF THE PRINCE OVER YOUR NATION

The nation of Israel was in an hour of great distress. The Philistines had gathered their armies together to battle against them. Little did Israel and their backslidden king realize that this attack of the enemy was all in God's perfect timing and was in accordance with His purpose and will. God was about to demonstrate His right arm of power and show Himself mighty on behalf of His children! He was going to use the lowly shepherd boy, David, that He had anointed with His power to accomplish what no man in the world could accomplish on his own. Israel had become proud of their natural ability under the leadership of the king that they had chosen over the divine leadership of God. Now God was about to reveal the truth that the prophet Zechariah would later pen: "...'Not by might nor by power, but by My Spirit,' says the Lord of hosts" (Zechariah 4:6).

JOHN ARCOVIO

After having been anointed by the prophet Samuel to be the future king, David returned to the daily duty of tending his father's sheep. Many times as he sat on the quiet hillsides, gently stroking his harp, the fleeting thoughts of discouragement and disillusion would fill his mind with questions. "What did God really say through His prophet? What did you really hear?" Now and then when David would visit Saul at the king's request, he would sit playing his harp wondering if the king really even noticed him at all. Nevertheless, David was able to curb his yearning to fill the clothes of potential and promise that had been prophetically tailored and laid out before him, and still faithfully fulfilled his daily tasks. "True," he reasoned within himself, "Samuel is God's anointed prophet and I believe God will fulfill all that He spoke of, but I must not get ahead of God's timing and pervert God's purpose with the efforts of my own ambitions."

Still, as he looked out over those sheep that he loved so dearly—so much so that he was willing to lay down his life for them—he could not shake the growing inner understanding that God had a much higher calling and plan for his life. Somehow David knew that the day would come that he would have to leave those precious sheep and fulfill the tremendous prophecy that rested upon him. While this understanding left an empty, sad feeling in David's heart, he also felt the excitement and anticipation that built as each day passed.

Meanwhile, on a mountain on one side of the valley of Elah, Saul and his proud, self-sufficient Israeli army gathered and pitched their tents. On the opposite side of the valley was the mountain upon which the Philistines gathered. The great valley of Elah stretched out between them, taunting and challenging the two armies to meet on its ground for the awful battle that was sure to ensue.

It had been so long since the men of Israel had seen their king build an altar and humble his heart before Jehovah that their hearts had become hardened and insensitive to the need of God's counsel for battle. Not one single whispered prayer went up as the men nervously waited for direction from their corrupted leader.

Suddenly the enormous figure of a man loomed over the top of the mountain on the Philistines' side. The men of Israel froze in disbelief at this muscle-bound champion of war as he sauntered toward the edge of the camp of Israel. Never before had their eyes witnessed such a powerful, menacing machine of destruction. This giant of a man, who they would find out later was Goliath of Gath, stood with both feet spread apart and drove his spear into the ground.

His height was six cubits and a span (approximately nine feet, nine inches). He had a bronze helmet on his head, and he was armed with a coat of mail, and the weight of the coat was five thousand shekels (125 pounds) of bronze. And he had bronze armor on his legs and a bronze javelin between his shoulders. Now the staff of his spear was like a weaver's beam, and his iron spearhead weighed six hundred shekels (fifteen pounds); and a shield bearer went before him (I Samuel 17:4-7).

Goliath stared straight into the shifting eyes of King Saul who could not return the challenge but looked away.

Then he stood and cried out to the armies of Israel, and said to them, "Why have you come out to line up for battle? Am I not a Philistine, and you the servants of Saul? Choose a man for yourselves, and let him come down to me. If he is able to fight with me and kill me, then we will be your servants. But if I prevail against him and kill him, then you shall be our servants and serve us." And the Philistine said, "I defy the armies of Israel this day; give me a man, that we may fight together" (I Samuel 17:8-10).

When Saul and his men heard these words, their hearts melted within them and they all began to tremble with fear. For forty days Goliath drew near and presented himself. Morning and evening every day he taunted, mocked and challenged the army of Israel and their God.

Jesse's three eldest sons had gone to fight the battle with Saul, while David would occasionally be requested of Saul to come and play his harp, then return to feed his father's sheep at Bethlehem. On each of David's trips to the king's palace, he had not heard any news about the war or the battle that was at hand.

One morning Jesse approached David as he was feeding the sheep and said to him, "Take thou for your brothers an ephah of this drying grain and these ten loaves and run to your brothers at the camp and carry these ten cheeses to the captain of the thousand and see how your brothers fare. And bring back news of them."

This opportunity greatly excited David. However, when he looked upon the face of his father he could see that he was concerned about his three sons and about sending another son so close to the battle.

Early the next morning, David rose, left the sheep with a keeper, packed the provisions for his brothers and left to fulfill this duty. Little did David know that God had ordained this occasion to fulfill His promise in David's life.

Allow me to note here that David would have never met Goliath on the battlefield if he had not realized that it was time to leave his beloved sheep with the keeper and move on to the greater challenge that God had set before him. David now had a giant to deal with and a battle to fight that would affect a nation.

Though we may be involved in God's service and love the work we are doing, when God calls us unto a greater challenge, we must be willing to leave our tasks behind and move into the new dimension of warfare God has for us.

As David walked along the dusty roads, crossing through the outcroppings of limestone and scraggly brush, he wondered, "Is Israel fighting? Are they winning? Are they losing? What will I encounter at the battlefield?"

Suddenly, as he came close to the army camp, he heard Israel's loud battle shout. David's heart beat faster and his pace quickened. He topped the hill and saw that Israel and the Philistines had drawn up in battle, army against army. David left the supplies with a keeper and ran to the army to greet his brothers. While he talked with them, from out of the Philistine army stepped a giant of a man, Goliath of Gath. Goliath spoke the same words that he had been speaking for forty days, taunting and challenging Israel to give him a man that could fight him in battle.

David was astonished as he watched his brothers and all of the other mighty warriors of Israel cower and look fearfully at each other. David was further shocked when he saw them all

turn back and flee to their tents. This greatly concerned David
for his valiant heart never knew the feeling of fleeing.

Later, as he sat by the fire mulling over this strange situation, he overheard some of the men of Israel talking quietly,
"Have you seen this man who has come up? Have you seen how
huge he is? Surely he has come to fight Israel." Another man
sitting despondently on the ground with his face in his hands
spoke, "There is not a man alive in our ranks that could take on
this giant of a man." One of the king's guards walked up and
spoke out saying, "Haven't you heard that the king has offered
that whoever kills this Philistine will be enriched with great
riches? Furthermore he will give him his own daughter and give
his father's house exemption from all of Israel's taxes." "So
what?" another man muttered. "It's still too small a reward to
lose your head over."

Then David approached the men and spoke up, "What shall
be done for the man who kills this Philistine and takes away this
reproach from Israel? For who is this uncircumcised Philistine
that he should defy the armies of the living God?" The men
turned and once again explained to David what the king was
offering for the head of this Philistine.

Eliab, David's oldest brother, overheard David speaking to
these men. He rushed over, spun David around and said,
"David, why have you come down here?" David looked at him
in astonishment. Before David could answer, Eliab accused him
and said, "Now who did you leave those few sheep in the wil-
derness with? I know your pride and the insolence of your
heart. You just simply came down to see the battle." David interrupted him and said strongly, "What have I done now? Is
there not a cause?" Then he turned from Eliab to the men and
repeated, "Is there not a cause?" He then turned to the whole

army and shouted out, "IS THERE NOT A CAUSE?" All of the men of Israel turned to avoid his gaze and muttered under their breath about this young, cocky, arrogant kid coming in and trying to tell them how to fight a battle.

Standing against a tent was one of the king's servants. He overheard David's bold statement, rushed back to Saul and reported to him the words that David had spoken. Saul then sent for David. As David approached Saul, David sensed that God was about to fulfill the purpose that he had for so long hoped, wished, and dreamed about. David looked Saul in the eye and said, "Let no man's heart fail because of that Philistine. Your servant will go and fight with Goliath."

Saul looked at David and laughed. "Ha! You are not able to go against this Philistine to fight with him for you are a youth and he is a man of war from his youth." David looked Saul right in the eye and replied, "There was a time when your servant used to keep his father's sheep that there came a lion once against the sheep and God delivered him into my hands. Later a bear came and again God delivered him into my hands. Just as by the help of God your servant has killed both the lion and the bear, this uncircumcised Philistine will be like one of them. Can't you see he has defied the armies of the living God? Moreover, the Lord, who delivered me from the paw of the lion and the paw of bear, will deliver me from the hand of this Philistine." Saul was shocked at this young man's boldness but decided, "What is there to lose? Go ahead, David, and the Lord be with you."

As David began to leave the room Saul suddenly stood and said, "Come back here, young man." David walked back and Saul said, "Here, put on my armor and take my sword." Saul put the bronze helmet on his head, clothed him with a coat of armor and fastened his own personal sword to the armor. David tried to walk but he felt clumsy. He had not tested these instruments of warfare. David turned back to Saul, handed him the bronze helmet and sword and said, "I cannot fight with these for I have not tested them." David reached down, took his staff in his hand—his trusted staff that had taken him through many battles and many, many years of protecting his father's sheep—and walked away into the valley of Elah.

In the valley was a running brook. David chose out of the brook five stones that had been polished smooth from the water's current. David put them in his shepherd's bag which he had carried for many years. He then took his sling, stood up and began to walk toward the camp of the Philistines.

When the Philistines looked up and saw that someone was finally coming to fight their champion, they left their tents and rushed forth to see who this person could be. Then Goliath's shield-bearer began to walk toward David.

When Goliath finally saw David, he disdained him and began to laugh and mock him. Here was only a young man, ruddy and good-looking, coming to fight *him*, the champion of the Philistines. He roared out, "Ha! Am I a dog that you come to me with sticks?" The Philistines began to curse and swear by their many gods against David. Then Goliath said to David, "Come here, little boy. I will give your flesh to the birds of the air and to the beasts of the field." David looked the Philistine in the eye and said back,

You come to me with the sword and the spear, and with the javelin, but I come to you in the name of the Lord of Hosts, the God of the armies of Israel whom you have defied. This day the Lord will deliver you into my hand and I will strike you and take your head from you. And this day I will give the carcass of the camp of the Philistines to the birds of the air and to the wild beasts of the field, that all the earth may know that there is a God in Israel. Then all this assembly shall know that the Lord does not save with sword and spear, the battle is the Lord's and he will give you into our hands (I Samuel 17:45-47).

This enraged Goliath and he rushed forward to deal what he thought would be the death blow to this little lad. When he rushed forward David also ran to meet him. Then David reached into his bag, took out a stone, loaded his trusted sling and slung it, striking the Philistine in his forehead. The stone sank deep into Goliath's forehead and he fell down on his face to the earth. David ran and took Goliath's sword out of its sheath and cut his head off.

When the Philistines saw that their champion was dead, they turned and fled. The men of Israel arose, shouted and pursued the Philistines as far as the entrance of the valley, even unto the gates of Akron. Along the way the wounded of the Philistines fell along the road to Shaaraim as far as Gath and Akron.

The Israelites returned from chasing the Philistines and plundered their tents. David took the head of Goliath and brought it to Jerusalem; he also put Goliath's armor in his tent.

With the completion of this battle, David's prophetic purpose was beginning to be fulfilled.

FIGHTING THE GIANT OF OUR NATION

You will notice that the first warfare is personal: that of the lion of the flesh. Either you are going to kill the lion or the lion is going to kill you. The second warfare is a battle for a church and for a city: the warfare of the bear or of the powers and authorities in your city and government.

The third warfare, the warfare of the giant, is a battle with the principality over your nation. This was reflected when David stepped onto the battleground with Goliath. This was a victory for the entire nation of Israel.

I believe all across America, God is raising anointed churches as epicenters of apostolic revival. These churches will face their lions and their bears, and they will dare to step out onto the battleground of the Goliath of this nation.

When David took his staff in his hand and went to the valley to choose the five smooth stones out of the brook, this was symbolic of David going into his personal valley. In the valley times of our soul, we can dig out what we need to win the warfare of the lion, bear and giant. Many times these valleys consist of struggle and misunderstanding. These are times when you hunger after God and simply walk with Him in the face of discouragement, persecution, and seeming defeat. Yes, here in this valley we will dig out what we need to face the giant of this generation.

David could not put on the armor that Saul gave him. When David stepped out onto the battlefield of the giant, he used the exact weapons he had used to defeat the lion and the bear. When we step out onto the battlefield of the prince of our nation, we are not going to step out with some newly invented weapon. We will use what we used back in the early humble times of warfare against the lion of our flesh and against the bear of our city. The same weapons of fasting, prayer, faith in

God's Word and obedience to His Spirit's leading are ᴜᴜᴄ weapons that will bring us the victory.

Just as David said, "You come to me with a sword and with a spear and with a javelin, but I come to you in the name of the Lord of Hosts, the God of armies of Israel whom you have defiled," we also can face the giants of our age in the all-powerful name of Jesus! My fellow laborer, do not feel pressured to try to discover some new weapon to fight these warfares. The name of Jesus is powerful enough to bring apostolic revival!

Paul spoke of this third dimension of warfare in Ephesians 6:12, "For you do not wrestle against flesh and blood, but against principalities...." *Principalities* is translated from *arche* (ark-hay') or "chief in series of leaders, the beginning, the origin or the source."

Every nation that man has set boundaries around such as the United States, Mexico, France, Libya, Russia and China has a demonically-appointed principality which commands all levels of power in the dark realm.

I believe that any church which has dealt with their lions and has broken the back of the bear of their city will see the Goliath of that nation come tumbling down. Through this victory they will cap the source of all demonic attacks in their nation, and this will allow the church to become the victorious, aggressive force that God has meant them to be in this last hour.

In Daniel 10:13 the angel told Daniel, "But the prince of the kingdom of Persia withstood me 21days and behold, Michael, one of the chief princes came to help me for I had been left alone there with the kings of Persia." I believe this referred to the ruling prince of the nation of Persia that had come against Daniel's 21 days of fasting and against the humbling of his heart in prayer. The prince had tried to obstruct the answer the angel was wanting to give to Daniel.

The angel further stated, "Do you know why I have come to you? Well, now I must return to fight with the prince of Persia and when I have gone forth indeed, the prince of Greece will come" (verse 20). So not only do we find reference in the Word of God to a prince over the nation of Persia, but also a prophetic statement about the prince of ancient Grecia that would later reign as the ruling force in the supernatural realm.

In I Corinthians 15:32 Paul said, "...in the manner of men I have fought with beast of Ephesus. What advantage is it to me?" Paul was speaking of the ruling prince at that point in time.

I believe that at the time a person or a church moves into the dimension of a *ten-to-twenty-one-day fast,* they are beyond the warfare of the flesh and even beyond warring against the bear of their city. They have entered the beginning stages of warfare on the battlefield of the prince over their nation.

Matthew 16:18-19 tells us how we should pray in the warfare of the giant.

And I also say to you that you are Peter, and on this rock I will build My church, and the gates of Hades shall not prevail against it. And I will give you the keys of the kingdom of heaven, and whatever you **bind on earth** will be **bound in heaven**, and whatever you **loose on earth** will be **loosed in heaven**.

Often when we are attacked spiritually, we hinder God from answering our prayers because we don't pray scripturally. If when we are under the attack of the enemy, we attempt to loose

God's power, gifts and angels without first binding the spirit of the attack, we are not praying scripturally. God commands us to first bind the spirit of the attack. Only after we have done so are we free to loose the Spirit to operate on our behalf. Simply praying and asking God to release mercy, anointing, or healing without first binding the spirit of the attack is to pray a power-less prayer.

If you are experiencing an attack against your finances, bind the spirit of that attack. If you are suffering from an attack on your character from other brethren, do what the Bible tells you to:

> Moreover if your brother sins against you, go and tell him his fault between you and him alone. If he hears you, you have gained your brother. But if he will not hear, take with you one or two more, that "by the mouth of two or three witnesses every word may be established." And if he refuses to hear them, tell it to the church. But if he refuses even to hear the church, let him be to you like a heathen and a tax collector. Assuredly, I say to you, whatever you **bind on earth** will be **bound in heaven,** and whatever you **loose on earth** will be **loosed in heaven** (Matthew 8:15-18).

Jesus closed this teaching on offense with a powerful principle: first bind the spirit of the attack and then loose God's power. Remember, when you are walking in the spirit realm the tallest trees will always catch the most wind. You can expect adversity, persecution and wrongdoings by the hands of brethren. We must realize that, when God allows those above you to wrong you and hurt you through cruel misunderstandings, He is using them to lift and exalt you.

Remember that Joseph was stripped of his coat of many colors when his brothers threw him into a dry well and later sold him as a slave. He was later lied on by Potiphar's wife and stripped of yet another coat. Joseph had to realize that those natural coats meant nothing compared to the dream that God was fulfilling.

Just because God has a plan for you does not necessarily mean that it will be fulfilled immediately. The will of man may hinder the will of God for a length of time. It was the will of God for Joseph to be prime minister over the whole nation, while it was the will of Joseph's brethren for Joseph to be a slave stripped of all honor. Joseph chose to have a right spirit; therefore for every door that man shut, God opened another. When man shut the door God opened, God opened yet another, until finally Joseph stepped out onto the platform of God's perfect will.

My friend, when God allows the coats of honor, reputation and prestige to be ripped from us, we must realize that He is using these events to strengthen, lift and exalt us. If we will simply choose the weapons of prayer and fasting and bind the spirit of the attack against us, then God will keep opening doors until we are in the middle of God's perfect will.

Maybe you are suffering in your body right now. Perhaps you have prayed and have believed for many months or years that God will heal you. You have released your faith and have loosed God to operate on your behalf through the gifts of healing and working of miracles. Right now, while you are reading this book, stand to your feet and bind the spirit of this attack. Bind the spirit of cancer in Jesus' name. Bind the spirit of diabetes in Jesus' name! Bind the spirit of the pain in your body in Jesus' name! Be loosed in the spirit of liberty even now as the gifts of healing begin to flow through your body. Go ahead, lift your hands and just praise Him for it. God is worthy!

Another scripture supporting this spiritual truth is Mark 4:35-41:

> On the same day, when evening had come, He said to them, "Let us cross over to the other side." Now when they had left the multitude, they took Him along in the boat as He was. And other little boats were also with Him. And a great windstorm arose, and the waves beat into the boat, so that it was already filling. But He was in the stern, asleep on a pillow. And they awoke Him and said to Him, "Teacher, do You not care that we are perishing?" **Then He arose and rebuked the wind**, and said to the sea, **"Peace, be still!"** And the wind ceased and there was a great calm. But He said to them, "Why are you so fearful? How is it that you have no faith?" And they feared exceedingly, and said to one another, "Who can this be, that even the wind and the sea obey Him!"

The first thing Jesus did was rebuke the wind. He bound the spirit of the attack that came against Him and His disciples. Then He loosed His peace and spoke the word of faith, saying, **"Peace, be still."**

It is time for us, as the sons and daughters of God, to realize that this is the hour of visitation of apostolic revival upon this nation. This is our day. Now is the time for God to pour His spirit out upon America as He has done in so many other nations. Paul wrote in Ephesians 3:8-10,

To me, who am less than the least of all the saints, this grace was given, that I should preach among the Gentiles the unsearchable riches of Christ, and to make all see what is the fellowship of the mystery, which from the beginning of the ages has been hidden in God who created all things through Jesus Christ; to the intent that now the manifold wisdom of God might be made known by the church to the principalities and powers in the heavenly places.

It is time for the church to let the prince in this nation know that he is *not* the ruling power of this nation. **"The earth is the Lord's and the fulness thereof..."** (Psalm 24:1). It is time for those that will dare to kill the lion of their flesh and see the back of the bear of their city broken, to step out by faith and with authority onto the battlefield of Goliath.

Though many ministry leaders have filled soccer stadiums with thousands, hoping to see the Goliath of their nation come tumbling down, we have seen the demise of these flaunted efforts because they never dealt with the lion and the bear in their own personal lives. Isaiah 57:12 tells us, "He who puts his trust in me, shall possess the land and shall inherit my holy mountain." It is time for us to inherit the mountain of God—to inherit what God has ordained for us. Jesus spoke in Matthew 12:28-29, "But if I cast out demons by the Spirit of God, surely the kingdom of God has come upon you. Or how can one enter a strong man's house and plunder his goods, unless he first binds the strong man? And then he will plunder his house."

We must first bind through prayer and fasting the lions, the bears and the Goliath of our nation. Then we can loose through faith the operation of God's spirit, angels and gifts across this land. **If we want to spoil the enemy's efforts in America, we**

must first bind the lion and the bear and then trust that God will destroy the yoke of the Goliath of this nation.

The Apostolic Church of Ethiopia is an excellent example of a church that, through prayer, fasting, faith and obedience, has destroyed the yoke of the lion of their flesh and the bear of their city and is now reaching for the Goliath of their nation. The fact that the church in Addis Ababa runs in excess of 5,000 is but a small testament to the fact that they have dared to challenge the bear of their city. Brother Teklemariam has always believed God for the millions in Ethiopia. He has successfully transmitted unto his saints his call and burden to evangelize the millions. As long as this church keeps everything together, they are well on their way to seeing the giant of Ethiopia defeated.

Once the enemy in one dimension has had his authority destroyed, he can not return at that same level of authority unless he first destroys the church that defeated him. This is due to the fact that as you reach a new level of warfare, your prayers take on new authority. The prayers that may have been non-effectual while fighting the lion are now gaining results in the warfare of the bear. Likewise, when you have defeated the bear, your prayers take on a new dimension while fighting the giant. Therefore, the defeated spirit of your city cannot come back to rule with the same power it once had unless it first destroys the church that took its authority in the first place.

I believe God chose David because in each stage of his life, he performed every task, no matter how small, as though his life depended on it. Thus we must place every temporal thing not linked to apostolic revival behind us. We must focus our efforts, vision and strength on seeing the Goliath of our nation defeated.

David was also chosen because he was aware of his hour of visitation. He was aware of when it was time to leave his dad's sheep. He was aware of when it was time to move beyond the lion and the bear and on to the greater challenge.

All those that had the power, training, and obligation to fight Goliath were cowering in their tents. They were waiting for somebody to step out and take action. David was not qualified to fight Goliath. He did not have the experience or the maturity necessary, nevertheless, **David hastened himself to meet this challenge.**

How long will we cower behind our excuses for non-productivity in our lives and ministries? How long will we cower behind empty pews in our churches? How long will we cower defenseless and powerless against the princes of our city? How many more conferences must go by with us strutting across the platform bragging that we have the greatest teachers and the greatest singers in the world? We offer this "smoke screen" of an excuse instead of truly **hastening ourselves** to meet the challenge of this hour!

We have been deceived by the pits of hell! The deceiver is attempting to get the church to focus on perfecting and refining our natural talents and abilities instead of focusing on what is really important: reaching, affecting and making a difference for the lost and hurting souls of this generation.

We do *not* have the greatest preachers and the greatest singers. What we have is Jesus. His anointing. His strength. His power! If anything is going to be done, it will be done because somebody chose to defeat the lion of his flesh, the bear of his city, and the Goliath of his nation.

We must not settle for the minimum of thinking that apostolic revival in America is just the perfection of what we already have. We dare not pat ourselves on the back and say with bloated egos, "We have the best."

The story is told of the evangelist who held a revival in a certain city. When the revival was over, somebody said to another, "What a great revival this was."

The second asked, "Oh? How many got the Holy Ghost?"

The first replied, "Well, no one got the Holy Ghost."

The second then asked, "Well, then, was anyone healed?"

"No, no one was healed."

"Was anybody delivered?"

The first answered, "No, but you should have heard his wife sing, and you should have heard him preach!"

To reduce apostolic revival down to this pitiful demonstration is a mockery in the sight of God. It is time for us to quit putting up smoke screens showing how great and grand we are. It is time to realize that somebody has got to get out onto Goliath's battlefield and face the challenge of this hour. Who will dare to step out?

This is the hour of visitation of apostolic revival and we must become aware of it! David hastened himself to meet the Philistine; likewise we must hasten ourselves to meet the challenges of this hour.

Luke 19:41-44 records a very sad time in the life of Jesus.

Now as He drew near, He saw the city and wept over it, saying, "If you had known, even you, especially in this your day, the things *that make* for your peace! But now they are hidden from your eyes. For days will come upon you when your enemies will build an embankment around you, surround you and close you in on every side, and level you, and your children within you, to the ground; and they will not leave in you one stone upon another, because you did not know the time of your visitation."

Jesus was weeping because they did not realize why He was there. The spiritually blind of that day were so caught up in their own traditions and self-righteousness, perfecting what they already had, that they missed the fact that the God of glory had come to visit in a special way and bring to them a brand new dimension of grace and salvation. We must not be caught sitting with our hands folded in complacency and self-satisfaction in this last hour while God is wanting to sweep this nation with apostolic revival. **Brothers and sisters, we must become aware of our time of visitation**.

The 1994 Ethiopian crusade broke and humbled me. I remember lying on my face on the concrete platform, weeping for over an hour. The tears pooled in a puddle around my face on the floor because I was so convicted by those precious Ethiopians' sacrifice and dedication. My spirit was oblivious to the threat of catching some virus or bug on that dirty floor. Their hunger for God and their willingness to obey the leading of His spirit so broke me that I vowed to God that I would change when I returned to America. I vowed that I would never stand behind a pulpit and brag about some sacrifice I had made in the past.

God has revealed to me that, for the fire of God's anointing and glory to fall, there must first be a **fresh sacrifice** on the altar. Anyone can build an altar and talk about it for many years, but **a fresh fire demands a fresh sacrifice!** God has allowed a fresh fire of commitment and consecration to light up in my soul. I now try to keep the fire burning through consistent communion with God and through a once-monthly all-night prayer meeting. **This is our day of visitation. Now is the time!**

As I mentioned in Chapter 2, the Apostolic Church of Ethiopia spends each Friday evening in all-night prayer. This has been going on for years and is one of the reasons why great revival has swept Ethiopia. This fact brought to my memory the many all-night Friday prayer meetings that I spent while sitting under the ministry of Brother James Kilgore at Life Tabernacle in Houston, Texas.

On that concrete floor in Ethiopia, I promised God that I would never again boast of those all-night prayer meetings in the past. I said, "God, I will not get behind the pulpit again and talk about those sacrifices of old. There will be a fresh fire!" Even now as I prepare to go on the 1995 Ethiopian crusade, I am asking God, "Lord, break me up again. Let the fallow ground of my soul again be broken. Allow me to once again become aware of this hour of the visitation of your glory that you are bringing to our world. Lord, allow me to again return to America and—regardless of who believes it or not—proclaim that this is our day of apostolic outpouring, that this is our hour!"

In the Spirit realm, timing is everything, and it is time for God to fulfill His prophetic promise and purpose in this land.

Luke 18:7-8 says, "And shall God not avenge His own elect who cry out day and night to Him, though He bears long with them? I tell you that He will avenge them speedily. Nevertheless, when the Son of Man comes, will He **really find faith on the earth**?"

Our heartfelt answer is, "Yes, Lord, by your grace and by your strength **you will find faith** in America to believe for this great move of your Holy Spirit which even now is sweeping our nation." **This is our day of visitation. Now is the time! We** must dare by faith to cross over the river Jordan and obtain the promise.

Paul wrote in Romans 8:37, "Yet in all these things we are more than conquerors through Him who loved us." How do we become conquerors? We become conquerors when we overcome the lion of our flesh, when we overcome the vices of sin in our life. We become conquerors when we see our churches turn to spiritual principles of apostolic revival. We become conquerors when we see the back of the bear of our cities broken and the Spirit of God beginning to move throughout those cities. **We become more than conquerors** when we face the giant and move on to possess the land.

Israel may have conquered Ai and Jericho, but so much of God's promised land was left unconquered because of Israel's disobedient unbelief. We must not fall prey to the common mistake of relaxing and no longer reaching for more just because a small victory was won. We must through faith become more than conquerors, cross over the Jordan, and obtain the promise that our nation will be affected by the Word and Spirit.

What will we be known for in this last hour? What will be recorded in history about us? Will we be remembered as having choked on the brink of our miracle? Will we be remembered as having missed the prophetic promises of God because of our unbelief, carnality and unwillingness to humbly submit to each other? Will we go down in history as being the finest singers and speakers in America or as being the children of God who dared to believe that our nation could be shaken for His cause?

Paul said in Romans 1:8, "First, I thank my God through Jesus Christ for you all, that your **faith is spoken of throughout the whole world.**"

When your name and reputation are discussed, what are you known for? Faith and godliness? Carnality and unbelief? Oh, God, let us be known as your faith-filled sons and daughters. Let our reputation go far and wide as being those who dare to believe, those who exercise faith, and those who will dare to cross over Jordan and obtain the promise of apostolic revival in America. **This is our day of visitation. Now is the time!**

The latter house of glory will be far greater than the former house. We are standing on the brink of a visitation of God's presence that will shut the mouths of mockers, scoffers, and those that would discredit. Those who have scoffed at the mighty move of God in Ethiopia, Asia and many other areas of the world will have to be silent.

I Peter 2:12 says, "Having your conduct honorable among the Gentiles, that when they speak against you as evildoers, they may, by your good works which they observe, **glorify God in the day of visitation.**" The enemy's manipulations, dirty politics and evil workings have been magnified all too long. It is time for the Kingdom of God to be magnified in our midst.

David said, "Oh, come magnify the Lord with me and let us exalt his name together" (Psalm 34:3). When something is magnified, it does not really become larger; it only appears larger. So how is God magnified? Through His working in people's lives. When the world observes God's mighty hand working in our lives, then God becomes magnified in the world's eyes.

We can talk all we want about the mighty miracles God is doing in some far-off country, but when the world observes us exercising the faith for the possessed to be delivered, for the blind to see, for the deaf to hear, for the lame to walk, for the dead to be raised, and for thousands to be filled with the Holy Ghost, then God will be magnified in their eyes.

For forty years Moses lived with feelings of failure, defeat, and self-pity. Then God called him to step out and lead Israel in the day of God's visitation of glory. Israel had cried out to God for 400 years for deliverance from the enemy's oppression. God bore long with them, but when He decided it was time, He delivered approximately six million people overnight. Yes, when God says it's time, He can perform the mightiest miracle in one day. **This is our day of visitation. Now is the time!**

In Exodus 18:8, Moses told his father-in-law Jethro all that the Lord had done to Pharaoh and to the Egyptians for Israel's sake. You see, for forty years Jethro had seen Moses cowering on the backside of the desert, yet all the while trying to convince Jethro about how great his God was. Nothing Moses could say could convince Jethro how awesome this Jehovah God that Moses served was.

After forty years, all it took to convince Jethro was one act of obedience. When Moses stepped from his burning bush experience to obey God, God could magnify Himself in the midst of the nations.

Then Jethro rejoiced for all the good which the Lord had done for Israel, whom He had delivered out of the hand of the Egyptians. And Jethro said, "Blessed be the Lord, who has delivered you out of the hand of the Egyptians and out of the hand of Pharaoh, and who has delivered the people from under the hand of the Egyptians. Now I know that the Lord is greater than all the gods; for in the very thing in which they behaved proudly, He was above them" (Exodus 18:9-11).

God became magnified through the simple obedience of one man. What could God do if several thousand in America would obey Him in this hour?

America has witnessed the demise of TV evangelists who have made a mockery out of Christianity and of the gifts of the spirit with their false gifts, deceptions, and hypocrisies. Additionally, for years moviegoers in American theaters have been subjected to films that portray God's power in a mocking fashion.

America, one day you will know that there is one true God. You will know that the true sons and daughters of this God are willing to step forth and meet the challenges of this hour. God will magnify Himself in the midst of America. It is time for us to allow God to become magnified in our lives. **This is our day of visitation. Now is the time!**

Acts 2:1-4 says,

When the Day of Pentecost had fully come, they were all with one accord in one place. And **suddenly** there came a sound from heaven, as of a rushing mighty wind, and it filled the whole house where they were sitting. Then there appeared to them divided tongues, as of fire, and one sat upon each of them. And they were all filled with the Holy Spirit and began to speak with other tongues, as the Spirit gave them utterance.

Suddenly is translated from *aphno* (af-no), meaning "unexpectedly." The book of Acts church was not expecting what took place when God poured His spirit out on the Day of Pentecost.

In this hour of complacency, many people will be caught unawares by the apostolic revival and the outpouring of the fire of the Holy Ghost. Jesus spoke in Luke 21:34, "But take heed to yourselves, lest your hearts be weighed down with carousing, drunkenness, and cares of this life, and that Day come on you **unexpectedly.**" I know this passage is used many times to illustrate the coming of the Lord, nevertheless, I believe Jesus could also have been speaking about our day of visitation catching us unawares.

Perhaps, Pastor, time and time again, you have hosted revival meetings, and have built your faith for revival in your city. Your have had your hopes high for a great breakthrough, only to find yourself facing the same struggles and battles as before. You have grown used to explaining to your people, "Yes, we have had a great meeting, but now it is time to return to the status quo, and continue to wait for our miracle."

My friend, I am here to tell you, now is the time. Dare to step out by faith. This is our day of visitation. It will happen. You will see revival in your city. You will see, as the lions of the flesh are put under control, and the back of the bear of your city is broken, that the Goliath of America's kingdom will come tumbling down.

In Luke 21:34, quoted above, the phrase *weighed down* is translated from the Greek *baruno* (bar-oo'-no) meaning "to be overcharged, to weigh down, burdened." *Cares* is translated from *merimna* (mer'-im-nah) or "through the idea of distraction; care, anxiety, distraction."

We live in the hour of distraction. Have you ever noticed how easy it is to become distracted from doing God's will and finishing His work? How quickly we can leave a red-hot prayer meeting and forget the burden we just felt so strongly! This is why Paul wrote in Philippians 3:13, "Brethren, I do not count myself to have apprehended; **but one thing I do**, forgetting those things which are behind and reaching forward to those things which are ahead...."

We must become focused like never before upon the need of this hour: the souls that are at stake. We must be aware of that God has placed us upon this terra firma to finish His work of redeeming lost mankind. We must safely guard the time, use it wisely and make it productive for the Kingdom of God. **My friend, again I tell you that this is our hour of visitation. Now is the time.**

The book of Numbers illustrates how God desires for His people to follow the leading of the Spirit in this day and time.

So it was always: the cloud covered it by day, and the appearance of fire by night. Whenever the cloud was taken up from above the tabernacle, after that the children of Israel would journey; and in the place where the cloud settled, there the children of Israel would pitch their tents. At the command of the Lord the children of Israel would journey, and at the command of the Lord they would camp; as long as the cloud stayed above the tabernacle they remained encamped. Even when the cloud continued long, many days above the tabernacle, the children of Israel kept the charge of the Lord and did not journey. So it was, when the cloud was above the tabernacle a few days: according to the command of the Lord they would remain encamped, and according to the command of the Lord they would journey. So it was, when the cloud remained only from evening until morning: when the cloud was taken up in the morning, then they would journey; whether by day or by night, whenever the cloud was taken up, they would journey. Whether it was two days, a month, or a year that the cloud remained above the tabernacle, the children of Israel would remain encamped and not journey; but when it was taken up, they would journey (Numbers 9:16-22).

For the past ten or fifteen years the cloud of apostolic revival has remained still. Oh, we have convinced ourselves that we will have revival in our city. We have convinced ourselves that we will have revival in our families. We believe that our lost husband, son or daughter will be restored back to the Kingdom of God. We believe God is going to move across America and that we will see thousands filled with the Spirit in one day. But we have also convinced ourselves that it is not yet time.

Here we sit, waiting for the cloud to move.

Church, the cloud is moving! It is time to journey into spiritual dimensions never before ventured. It is time to follow the leading of the Holy Spirit.

During the outpouring of the former rain in the book of Acts, the church adjusted its lifestyle to fit the moving of God's Spirit. Do we actually think that in this hour of the latter rain, while God is moving with great signs and wonders across the world, that He will wait until we can fit Him into our time schedules? We must respond *now* to this challenge!

With the coming of the year 2000, we will see four things accomplished that are relevant to the timing of God's operation. We will see the end of a decade (ten years), the end of a century (100 years), the end of a millennium (1000) years, and I believe we will see the end of a dispensation—the sixth dispensation of grace.

Genesis 2:2 teaches that for six days God worked, but on the seventh He rested. No, I am not saying that the coming of Christ will be in the year 2000, but I do believe that God is about to rest from His works in this hour. I believe that God is about to usher in this apostolic revival that He has promised us for so many years. We will see series of meetings where literally thousands will be filled with the Holy Ghost. Not just hundreds, but thousands, right here in the United States of America. It is time to rejoice, Church. It is time to step out by faith and obtain this promise.

4

THE THREE FEASTS

In Exodus 23, three feasts are described. These three feasts are types that point to where we stand in this last hour of God's great visitation. We as "blood bought, blood washed, spirit filled" children of God have already celebrated the first two feasts in accordance with God's plan. It is now time to celebrate the third and final feast.

I want to say at the outset of this discussion that, truly, Jesus is the fulfillment of all the feasts. He spoke in Matthew 5:17, "Do not think that I came to destroy the Law or the Prophets. I did not come to destroy but to fulfill."

Let us now look into these three feasts that God commanded His people to celebrate.

Three times you shall keep a feast to Me in the year: You shall keep the Feast of Unleavened Bread (you shall eat unleavened bread seven days, as I commanded you, at the time appointed in the month of Abib, for in it you came out of Egypt; none shall appear before Me empty); and the Feast of Harvest, the firstfruits of your labors which you have sown in the field; and the Feast of Ingathering at the end of the year, when you have gathered in the fruit of your labors from the field (Exodus 23:14-16).

The Feast of Unleavened Bread (also known as the Feast of Passover) was held as a tribute to the deliverance from the death angel when the blood was applied to the doorposts and lintel at the commandment of the Lord. The Feast of Harvest (or the Feast of Pentecost), which celebrated the firstfruits of their labors, was the commemoration of the giving of the law. The third feast was the Feast of the Ingathering (or the Feast of Tabernacles). It celebrated the complete harvest of the field.

THE FEAST OF PASSOVER

In our Christian lives today, we have already celebrated the Feast of Passover. We were delivered from the death angel of sin when the Lord became our Passover lamb, according to I Corinthians 5:7-8:

Therefore purge out the old leaven, that you may be a new lump, since you truly are unleavened. For indeed **Christ, our Passover**, was sacrificed for us. Therefore let us keep the feast, not with old leaven, nor with the leaven of malice and wickedness, but with the unleavened bread of sincerity and truth.

When we repent of our sins, when we truly determine to turn our back on our sinful ways and we are baptized in the precious name of Jesus, those sins are exonerated. We discover that God literally removes from us the old carnal man that we used to be, and He puts upon us His love, His forgiveness, His righteousness, His purity and His holiness. We actually become clothed with divine nature! This is why Paul wrote in Galatians 3:26-27, "For you are all sons of God through faith in Christ Jesus. For as many of you as were **baptized into Christ** have **put on Christ**."

When we through faith and obedience believe that Jesus Christ became our Passover Lamb and when we have the blood applied through baptism in Jesus' name, **we literally put on Christ.** You may have looked in a mirror to see only a failure with a multitude of weaknesses, but you must realize that you are not the person that you used to be. You are not a failure! You have been literally transformed by the power of God through putting on Christ.

II Corinthians 5:16-17 says,

Therefore, from now on, we regard no one according to the flesh. Even though we have known Christ according to the flesh, yet now we know Him thus no longer. Therefore, if anyone is in Christ, he is a **new creation; old things have passed away; behold, all things have become new.**

Peter further supports this revelation in I Peter 1:22-24:

Since you have purified your souls in obeying the truth through the Spirit in sincere love of the brethren, love one another fervently with a pure heart, having been born again, not of corruptible seed but incorruptible, through the word of God which lives and abides forever, because "All flesh is as grass, And all the glory of man as the flower of the grass. The grass withers, and its flower falls away, but the word of the Lord endures forever." Now this is the word which by the gospel was preached to you.

When we obey God's Word and put on Christ we partake of that incorruptible seed. We become born again through water and through spirit.

This truth is again supported in II Peter 1:4: "By which have been given to us exceedingly great and precious promises, that through these you may be partakers of the divine nature, having escaped the corruption that is in the world through lust."

Jesus Christ was the image of the invisible God, the "flesh of the eternal God."

Giving thanks to the Father who has qualified us to be partakers of the inheritance of the saints in the light. He has delivered us from the power of darkness and conveyed us into the kingdom of the Son of His love, in whom we have redemption through **His blood, the forgiveness of sins. He is the image of the invisible God**, the firstborn over all creation. For by Him all things were created that are in heaven and that are on earth, visible and invisible, whether thrones or dominions or principalities or powers. All things were created through Him and for Him. And He is before all things, and in Him all things consist. And He is the head of the body, the church, who is the beginning, the firstborn from the dead, that in all things He may have the preeminence. For it pleased the Father that in Him all the fullness should dwell, and by Him to reconcile all things to Himself, by Him, whether things on earth or things in heaven, having made peace through the blood of **His cross**. And you, who once were alienated and enemies in your mind by wicked works, yet now **He has reconciled in the body of His flesh through death**, to present you holy, and blameless, and above reproach in His sight (Colossians 1:12-22).

When you repent of your sins and are baptized in the precious name of Jesus, your sins are completely obliterated, not just put away in "File 13" so that when you make your first mistake, the enemy can drag them out to condemn you. Romans 8:1 says, "There is therefore now no condemnation to those who are **in Christ Jesus**, who do not walk according to the flesh, but according to the Spirit."

How do you get *in Christ Jesus?* You get in Christ Jesus when you put on Christ through water baptism in Jesus' name!

The moment you step out to try to be used of God, the enemy will whisper in your ear, "Who do you think you are, trying to be a vessel of God's power? Don't you remember all of your past mistakes? Have you forgotten about your closet full of the skeletons of your failures? Just try to step out and be used by God, and I will throw open that door and reveal to everyone the loser you really are!"

My friend, when old Slewfoot tries to drag up your past, you need to realize that your closet no longer holds the skeletons of your past, but they have been replaced by the trophy of God's grace and mercy! No matter what mistakes and failures the past held, we serve an ever merciful God! His mercies are afresh and new at the dawning of each day. Lamentations 3:22-23 says, "Through the Lord's mercies we are not consumed, because His compassions fail **not. They are new every morning**; Great is Your faithfulness." One thing you can always count on is God's finished work at Calvary! There is no past failure so great that God's infinite mercy cannot overcome it today.

Throw that closet wide open. Allow the world to see the trophy that the grace of God has made out of your weaknesses, failures and mistakes. The trophy is there because you have put on Christ! Go ahead, step out by faith, lay hands on the sick with authority! Teach that Bible study with anointing! Speak the Word of Faith with powerful prophetic results! You are a child of God! Royal blood flows through your veins! You are pure because He is pure. You are Holy and blameless for He is Holy and blameless.

Look again at Colossians 1:21-22 in the light of this glorious revelation: "And you, who once were alienated and enemies in your mind by wicked works, yet now He has reconciled in the body of His flesh through death, to present you **holy,** and **blameless,** and **above reproach in His sight."**

Not only are you above reproach in the sight of our ever faithful God, but also in the sight of the enemy, although he doesn't want to admit it.

The devil would like you to think he is observing you in your faults and flaws. What he really sees is the blood of Jesus, a constant reminder of his worst defeat: Calvary. He sees the powerful result of what has happened to your life since you put on Christ. The enemy only **remembers** your past mistakes and wants you to remember them as well. Why should we remember something God has completely forgotten and has even put away from His very presence? "As far as the east is from the west, so far has He removed our transgressions from us" (Psalm 103:12).

God does not see your mistakes and failures; He only sees His blood that He applied to your life when you obeyed His word, were baptized in Jesus' name, put on Christ, and became a trophy of His grace.

Yes, we have experienced our Passover and we need to celebrate it. We ought to thank God over and over for our deliverance from the death angel of sin and rejoice every day for the power of His cleansing blood. We should never forget the pit of sin God dug us from.

THE FEAST OF PENTECOST

Fifty days after the Feast of Passover was the Feast of Pentecost. Fifty days after the crucifixion of our Lord was the Day of Pentecost, where the firstfruits of this apostolic revival were gathered.

As the children of God today we have also celebrated the Feast of Pentecost. We've had our conferences and our revivals —our "feasts," if you will—celebrating the fact that we have been filled with the very presence and power of God with the evidence of speaking in other tongues. This is good. We should celebrate the Feast of Pentecost. We should venerate in the day we became born again, when God divinely filled us with His Spirit. This is the exact experience that took place on the Day of Pentecost in Acts 2:1-4.

When the Day of Pentecost had fully come, they were all with one accord in one place. And suddenly there came a sound from heaven, as of a rushing mighty wind, and it filled the whole house where they were sitting. Then there appeared to them divided tongues, as of fire, and one sat upon each of them. And they were all filled with the Holy Spirit and began to speak with other tongues, as the Spirit gave them utterance (or the ability to speak).

Later we discover in verse 13 that there were those who mocked and said that those in the upper room were full of new wine.

But Peter stood up and raised his voice and said to them, "Men of Judah and all who dwell in Jerusalem, let this be known to you and heed my words. For these are not drunk as you suppose, seeing it is only the third hour of the day. But this is what was spoken by the prophet Joel, 'And it shall come to pass in the last days, said God, I will pour out my spirit on all flesh. And your sons and your daughters shall prophesy. And your young men shall visions and your old men shall dream dreams. And on my menservants and on my maid servants I will pour out my spirit in those days and they shall prophesy'" (verses 14-18).

Yes, we have rejoiced in our Pentecost. We have rejoiced in our harvest of first fruits. We must remember though, it is only our *first fruits*. This is not the actual endtime harvest. It is not yet the harvest that God purposed prophetically for this hour. No matter how good a revival we have experienced in America, it is still only the final remnant of the Feast of Pentecost, the first fruits of our labors. We are soon to enter the actual harvest of our labors.

THE FEAST OF THE INGATHERING

I am thankful for the day when I was nine that God filled me with the baptism of the Holy Spirit and I began to speak in an unknown language as the Spirit of God gave me the ability to speak. At that young age, I could not fully understand nor appreciate the profound beauty of this experience as I do now at the age of 30. Nevertheless, it is as real today as it was 21 years ago!

We have celebrated long enough the Feast of Pentecost. It is time for the sons and daughters of God to enter into the celebration of the Feast of Tabernacles or the Feast of the Ingathering. It is time to begin, by faith, to rejoice for the millions that will experience the death, burial and resurrection of our Lord Jesus Christ through repentance, water baptism in the precious name of Jesus and the infilling of the Holy Spirit.

Right now, if you are reading this book and you have never experienced the baptism of the Holy Spirit evidenced with speaking in an unknown language, lift your hands and begin to believe now that you will receive this precious gift and become part of the rejoicing of the Feast of Tabernacles! If you will follow these next few simple steps, you will be guaranteed the opportunity to receive the infilling of the Holy Spirit even as thousands are now receiving it as you read.

First, relax. You cannot receive the Holy Spirit if you are uptight or fearful of this experience. You must understand that as you obey God and exercise your faith, God will cause His Spirit to become supernaturally birthed within you and you will begin to speak words you have never heard or spoken before.

Secondly, you must, from your heart, not your head, truly repent of your sins. Talk to God and tell Him you are truly sorry for committing these sins, that you purpose to turn your back on all sin and that you will endeavor to walk a Christian walk by power of the Holy Spirit He is about to fill you with. Understand that when you sincerely ask God to forgive you, you will be forgiven! It is that simple. You don't have to beg Him for hours. Go ahead, lay this book aside and take a few minutes to repent.

Third, you must now be truly ready for and want the infilling of God's Spirit. Be sure you are in an area where you will not be easily interrupted or distracted, though if you are truly desirous of His Spirit, God can fill you in the middle of the noisiest environment. Now, are you ready? The most exciting experience you will ever know is just about to happen! Lift your hands toward heaven and begin to praise the Lord with expressions such as, "I love You, Jesus," "Hallelujah, I praise You, Lord," or whatever you feel flowing from your heart in thankfulness and adoration. Allow the Spirit of God to be released in your life and **speak out by faith** the words God is creating within you. Go ahead, don't be afraid or embarrassed if you do not understand the words you are speaking. Speak them out in Jesus' name! Remember, you can only speak in one language at a time, so sometime you must let go of the English language you have spoken for so many years and let the Holy Ghost speak the heavenly language through you!

Please feel free to contact our ministry at the address at the front of this book if you have any questions or have just received the baptism of the Holy Spirit. We would love to hear from you!

Leviticus 23:40-41 says,

And you shall take for yourselves on the first day the fruit of beautiful trees, branches of palm trees, the boughs of leafy trees, and willows of the brook; and you shall rejoice before the Lord your God for seven days. You shall keep it as a feast to the Lord for seven days in the year. It shall be a statute forever in your generations. You shall celebrate it in the seventh month.

This is our day of visitation. Now is the time! It is time to rejoice in the Feast of the Ingathering. It is time to rejoice in the harvest that God is bringing to America. It is time to rejoice for that lost loved one that is coming in. When you rejoice, picture that loved one dancing and rejoicing with you, filled with and delivered by the power of the Holy Ghost. It will happen.

There may be some of us that have spent time weeping and travailing for souls. And yes, we must weep and travail for souls. But we must also know the joy of the Lord in rejoicing by faith for the harvest. We can rejoice because our God rejoices over us. "The Lord your God in your midst, The Mighty One, will save; He will **rejoice** over you with gladness, He will quiet you with His love, He will **rejoice** over you with singing" (Zephaniah 3:17).

Rejoice is translated from *suws* (soos) or *siys* (sece) meaning "rejoice, glad, greatly joy, make mirth, to exult, rejoice, or display joy. To spin around and to be glad."

This is how the Lord desires to behave in our midst when He sees the harvest being gathered. Luke 15:10 says, "Likewise, I say to you, there is joy in the presence of the angels of God over one sinner who repents." The reason the angels rejoice when one soul is reaped in endtime harvest is because they see their "Boss" rejoicing and they can do no less than what He does! We also should rejoice with Him. Don't ever let the devil condemn you for, or rob you of, your right to rejoice in the presence of God.

One of the most beautiful sights I have ever seen was during the Ethiopian crusade in March 1994. When the bus carrying our team pulled up to the crusade area, there were thousands of people lined up for over a hundred yards leaping in the air and rejoicing in God. I stood in awe as these joyous Ethiopians continuously rejoiced. Many of them were facing either persecution, poverty, starvation, or apparent death. But they rejoiced and rejoiced and worshiped and worshiped.

Some of the most beautiful sounds in Ethiopia were the drums beating at night as people with torches marched back to their tents. Sounds of praise and rejoicing went on throughout the night.

During our eight-hour bus trip through Ethiopia, precious

Ethiopian sisters and brethren on the bus clapped their hands, sang songs and rejoiced. Yes, rejoicing is part of this last day visitation. It is time for us to rejoice by faith for the Feast of the Ingathering.

John 4:34-38 says,

> Jesus said to them, "My food is to do the will of Him who sent Me, and to finish His work. Do you not say, 'There are still four months and then comes the harvest'? Behold, I say to you, lift up your eyes and look at the fields, for they are already white for harvest! And he who reaps receives wages, and gathers fruit for eternal life, that both he who sows and he who reaps may rejoice together. For in this the saying is true: 'One sows and another reaps.' I sent you to reap that for which you have not labored; others have labored, and you have entered into their labors."

Brother Teklemariam has told me how the large majority of the revival in Ethiopia has been amongst the young people. He also said that much of the revival has been harvested from fields they did not plow or sow in. Thousands have come from denominational churches. These people have been hungry for God's Spirit, desiring more of the whole counsel of God.

Brother Teklemariam told me that much persecution has come from these other church denominations. Many from the Denominational churches have beaten saints of the Apostolic Church of Ethiopia. Many have burned the Apostolic churches down. The Apostolic Church can no longer build a church out of wood or brush because of the threat of it being burned down. The majority of the churches are built out of steel or brick and clay.

This opened my eyes to what the scripture meant when it said that we reap in fields where we did not labor. I believe that in America there are millions of people that have a true walk with

God. They truly love Him and are serving Him to their fullest understanding. I also believe that God is bringing this great apostolic revelation unto them. This is part of our last day outpouring.

We must not compromise this message, or allow its beauty to become filtered. We must stand strong, and God will draw the millions that are hungry for truth. He will draw them to a deeper relationship and walk with Him. We must stand and boldly proclaim the truth of the death, burial and resurrection of our Lord Jesus Christ like we have never proclaimed it before.

Yes, part of this last day revival will be the unity of the message along with the unity of purpose among God's people who will exhibit a spirit of humility and submission.

Consider the disunity that man has contended with ever since the Tower of Babel.

Now the whole earth had one language and one speech. And it came to pass, as they journeyed from the east, that they found a plain in the land of Shinar, and they dwelt there. Then they said to one another, "Come, let us make bricks and bake them thoroughly." They had brick for stone, and they had asphalt for mortar. And they said, "Come, let us build ourselves a city, and a tower whose top is in the heavens; let us make a name for ourselves, lest we be scattered abroad over the face of the whole earth." But the Lord came down to see the city and the tower which the sons of men had built. And the Lord said, "Indeed the people **are one** and they all have **one language**, and this is what they begin to do; now nothing that they propose to do will be withheld from them. Come, let Us go down and there **confuse their language, that they may not understand one another's speech.**" So the Lord scattered them abroad from there over the face of all the earth, and they ceased building the city. Therefore its name is called Babel, because there the **Lord confused the language of all the**

earth; and from there the Lord scattered them abroad over the face of all the earth (Genesis 11:1-9).

Ever since the Tower of Babel debacle, not only have the earth's languages been confused, but the concepts of God have also been confused. Many have left Babel saying that there are three gods, five gods, or a thousand gods. Baal is god. Nature is god. You are a god. There is no god.

Part of this last hour revival will be the fulfilling of Zephaniah's prophecy: "For then I will restore to the peoples a **pure language,** that they all may call on the name of the Lord, to serve Him with one accord" (Zephaniah 3:9).

I believe that God is moving beyond the land of Ethiopia to bring this entire world, including America, into the spirit of unity and revival. We will realize the power of speaking the same message: the death, burial and resurrection of Jesus Christ. One of the greatest threats to the enemy's kingdom is the unity of the church.

Jesus gave a warning in Matthew 24:3-5.

Now as He sat on the Mount of Olives, the disciples came to Him privately, saying, "Tell us, when will these things be? And what will be the sign of Your coming, and of the end of the age?" And Jesus answered and said to them: "Take heed that no one deceives you. For many will come in My name, saying, **'I am the Christ**,' and will deceive many."

Jesus was not talking about many coming and saying that they were "the Christ." If someone put a robe on and walked the streets of America proclaiming he was "Christ," most Americans would only think he was crazy. (A few might follow, as those who followed Jim Jones or David Koresh.)

Jesus was talking about this day where many have

deceived millions by coming in His name and saying, "Jesus is the Christ," but teaching a perverted message that does not match the original. Paul wrote,

> But even if we, or an angel from heaven, preach any other gospel to you than what we have preached to you, let him be accursed. As we have said before, so now I say again, if anyone preaches any other gospel to you than what you have received, let him be accursed (Galatians 1:8-9).

I believe that just as the Ethiopians who were hungry for God came by the thousands, those here in America that truly hunger for the pure truth of God's Word will come and find it. They are hungry for His Word, and for the operation of God's Spirit.

There are those today, however, who have this truth and are foolish enough to let go of it in this last hour. They are watering down their doctrine and compromising their standards. These people are caught in a great big whirlpool of deception that is slowly pulling and sucking down millions. This great whirlpool will end up in the lap of that mother harlot, the Catholic church. Paul wrote in II Thessalonians 2:8-12,

> And then the lawless one will be revealed, whom the Lord will consume with the breath of His mouth and destroy with the brightness of His coming. The coming of the lawless one is according to the working of Satan, with all power, signs, and lying wonders, and with all unrighteous deception among those who perish, **because they did not receive the love of the truth,** that they might be saved. And for this reason **God will send them strong delusion,** that they should believe **the lie,** that they all may be condemned who did not **believe the truth but had pleasure in unrighteousness.**

We must love and preserve truth!

Those that will dare stand for and love truth will resist this strong delusion that God has divinely ordained for those who do not love it.

Paul wrote in II Corinthians 11:1-4,

> Oh, that you would bear with me in a little folly—and indeed you do bear with me. For I am jealous for you with godly jealousy. For I have betrothed you to one husband, that I may present you as a chaste virgin to Christ. But I fear, lest somehow, as the serpent deceived Eve by his craftiness, so your minds may be corrupted from the simplicity that is in Christ. For if he who comes **preaches another Jesus whom we have not preached**, or if you receive a **different spirit** which you have not received, or a **different gospel** which you have not accepted—you may well put up with it!

You see, there is not "another Jesus." We must preach the One true God whose name is Jesus!

God in this great hour of visitation is calling us, the true sons and daughters of God, the people of His name, to arise and proclaim His message like never before. All who will fight against this move of God will have the fear of God fall upon them. God will cause this great message to be spread across this nation in a mighty way.

A beautiful thing happened during the Ethiopian crusade in March 1994. I was thoroughly exhausted from my trip. I had endured about 24 hours of flying time and my body clock was all backwards. Every morning God would awaken me at 4:30 to rise and pray. The compound where we were staying had approximately one hundred huts scattered over a twenty-acre area. The only locations I had learned were where my hut was and where we had our meals.

On Saturday morning I was awakened by the presence of

God at 4:30. As I stepped out into the living area of this small hut, I knelt down and began to pray. The Lord spoke to me and said, "I want you to go to Brother Teklemariam's hut. He will talk to you about persecution." I arose from my knees and stepped out into the pitch black Ethiopian night. I was disoriented and did not know where I was.

I looked around me and as my eyes adjusted to the darkness I could make out the figure of a soldier standing nearby with a machine gun. Our huts were guarded day and night by soldiers with machine guns because of the threat of rebels in that area. I walked up to this man and said to him in English, "Sir, can you tell me where Teklemariam's hut is?" The guard looked at me and spoke back in an Ethiopian dialect, and I knew he could not understand what I was saying. So I turned back around and I whispered in prayer, "God, you are going to have to help me find his hut. I don't know where he is and I don't know where I am."

Suddenly I felt a strong impression of God's Spirit and I began to walk down a certain path. I walked for perhaps close to 150 yards till I came to a fork in the path. I felt impressed to take the right path. I began to walk down that path, then came to another fork. My impression led me down the left path. I walked again for another forty yards till I came to a three-way split. I felt impressed to take the third leg.

I walked along and found one small hut with a light on. I tiptoed up onto the porch, pulled back a shade and looked through the window. There was Brother Teklemariam laying fully clothed on his bed with his Bible across his chest. I tapped very lightly on the door so as not to wake him if he was asleep. He was awake, however, for God had already impressed him that I was going to come and talk to him.

When I walked into the room he said, "Brother Arcovio, open your Bible to II Timothy 3:10-12." I read,

But you have carefully followed my doctrine, manner of life,

107

purpose, faith, longsuffering, love, perseverance, persecutions, afflictions, which happened to me at Antioch, at Iconium, at Lystra—what persecutions I endured. And out of them all the Lord delivered me. Yes, and all who desire to live godly in Christ Jesus will suffer persecution.

We began to pray and God's Spirit moved into that room and such a mighty, beautiful way. Then Brother Teklemariam began to talk to me in quiet tones about the persecutions that he, his family and the church had suffered for the mighty name of Jesus. After thirty or forty minutes of discussing different persecutions, he began to talk about how the fear of God was beginning to sweep the nation. He told me how the wrath and judgment of God was beginning to fall against those of denominational beliefs who were persecuting the church, beating the saints and burning churches down. All across the country, the warning was spread to leave the Apostolic Church alone, because God would kill all who dared come against it.

Yes, the fear of God is our heritage. David wrote in Psalm 61:5, "For You, O God, have heard my vows; You have given me the heritage of those who fear Your name."

In the midst of authoring this book, I attended the 1995 crusade in Wara, Ethiopia, where God once again confirmed His Word with signs following. Approximately 80,000 people were filled with the baptism of the Holy Ghost. Hundreds of thousands were healed by the power of the name of Jesus. This is truly a nation that has entered the battlefield of Goliath. All efforts by the witch doctors, communists, the Coptic Church and other religious groups to hinder the crusade have been powerless. To date (October 1998) over 400,000 have received the Holy Ghost evidenced by speaking in other tongues in these crusades.

In 1992, the first year the Wara crusade was held, the area witch doctors decided to sacrifice nine bulls to place a curse on the Apostolic Church so that it would not grow. (As seven is the perfect number for Christians, nine is the perfect number for witch doctors.)

The first bull was killed and the fat was stretched out for the witch doctors to read the curse thereon. This reading showed that Wara conference was fenced in, protected by angels. The second bull's fat showed that thousands of people would come into this fenced area and be blessed of God. The third through eighth bulls' fat showed that nothing could stop this powerful crusade.

When they killed the last bull and read its fat, the witch doctors became very frightened by what they saw and would not repeat it. After much persuasion, they revealed that the last fat read that whoever fought against this great conference, God would kill.

As a result, most of the witch doctors have moved out of the area. In this year's conference there were four converted witch doctors who had been filled with the Holy Ghost in the 1994 crusade. The people have renamed "Wara" to "Wara Bethel" in honor of what God is doing there.

The area where the crusade is held is an eighty-acre clearing, the only clearing for many miles. The natives of the area cannot explain this mysterious clearing, for it was not cleared by man, but prepared by God for the crusade. The cool breeze, unobstructed because of the absence of trees, is free to blow through to keep the people cool during the crusade.

The clearing is big enough to hold up to five million people. Brother Teklemariam is believing God for fifty-four million people to eventually attend the Wara crusade and be filled with the spirit. God grant us greater vison!

EPILOGUE

As we stand on the brink of great apostolic revival in this last hour, perhaps you are still attempting to tack the lion skin of your flesh to the wall of your spiritual house. Or maybe you are attempting to break the back of the bear, the ruling authority in your city. Or you might be standing on the brink of joining the great army that God is raising across America that will dare to come against Goliath, the giant of our nation.

Hang in there and realize, the battle is not really ours, it is the Lord's. **This is our day of visitation. Now is the time!**

This may be the last book that God will ever allow me to write, but let it go down in history that this man of God was not caught unawares during this great hour of our visitation.

I want to boldly proclaim: Now is the time. Let us arise, kill the lion, hang the bearskin up and dare to believe that the Goliath in this nation will come tumbling down!

May the Lord richly bless you with strength, wisdom and courage in these three warfares.

OTHER MATERIALS BY JOHN ARCOVIO

The Way of the Eagle
Spiritual principles and the operation of spiritual gifts are illustrated through this fascinating portrait of an eagle in the wild. You will mount up with the wings of an eagle as you read. (Available in Spanish)

$12.00 each includes shipping

Three Warfares
Before genuine apostolic revival will ever sweep across our nation, the American Church will have to come to grips with three dimensions of spiritual warfare. Arm yourself and charge headlong into the battle as you read this book

$12.00 each includes shipping

The Mantle of God
The prophets of old were identified and protected by the unique mantle they
wore. Discover the New Testament believer's mantle, made also for identification and protection. Take it upon you as you read and wear it to the glory of God!

$12.00 each includes shipping

Discerning the Spirits of this End-Time Apostolic Age
As the coming of the Lord approaches and we prepare to cross the threshold into the 21st century, it is my conviction that the church must possess the operation of the gift of discerning of spirits that Paul wrote about in 2 Corinthians 12:10. This book will enlighten you in the area of discernment of the spirits of this hour.

$12.00 each includes shipping

The Other Side of Pentecost
The Other Side of Pentecost is a compilation of humorous stories that John Arcovio has heard, observed, or experienced while ministering in churches around the world. May this lighthearted look at Pentecost serve you much medicine.

$10.00 each includes shipping

Thoughts From Above
An eight-tape series dealing with prayer, fasting, the operation of spiritual gifts, and principles concerning the fivefold ministry.

$35.00 each includes shipping

Thoughts From Above Part II
An six-tape series dealing with principles concerning apostolic authority , an in-depth questions and answers session concerning the fivefold ministry and the spirit realm.

$35.00 each includes shipping

Personal Evangelism 101 Soulwinning Seminar
A "one-on-one ministry" Soulwinning seminar that will challenge your faith
and stir your heart to a greater burden for the lost. Comes with a 90-minute
cassette tape and a 16-page, easy-to-follow booklet. (Available in Spanish)

$15.00 each includes shipping

Visit our Web Site at http://www.spiritled.org

Please use order form on next page.

Order Form

Quantity	Description	Unit Price	Total
	The Way of the Eagle	$12.00	
	Three Warfares	$12.00	
	The Mantle of God	$12.00	
	Discerning the Spirits	$12.00	
	The Other Side of Pentecost	$10.00	
	Thoughts From Above	$35.00	
	Thoughts From Above II	$25.00	
	101 Ministry Seminar	$15.00	
		Extra Shipping and Handling	
		Grand Total	

All prices include shipping & handling. (Please add **5% of total materials ordered** for quantities of two or more. Add **20% for Next Day Air**.
Call for special wholesale price on book quantities over 20 or Tape quantities over 5.

Canadian and foreign shipments add **25% of total materials ordered** for all tape orders. **U.S. Currency only please**.
For credit card orders please call................. **1-800-839-2533**

Make check or money order payable to **Spirit Led Ministries, Inc.**
Spirit Led Ministries, Inc., 3422 W. Hammer Lane, Suite C-289
Stockton, CA 95219   (209)608-3399 or (209)478-8972 fax

Name: _____

Address:_____

City: _____

State: _____   Zip:_____

Phone: _____